U.S. IMPERIALISM AND PROGRESSIVISM

1896 to 1920

DOCUMENTING AMERICA
THE PRIMARY SOURCE DOCUMENTS OF A NATION

U.S. IMPERIALISM AND PROGRESSIVISM

1896 to 1920

EDITED BY JEFF WALLENFELDT, MANAGER, GEOGRAPHY AND HISTORY

Britannica®
Educational Publishing

IN ASSOCIATION WITH

ROSEN
EDUCATIONAL SERVICES

Published in 2013 by Britannica Educational Publishing
(a trademark of Encyclopædia Britannica, Inc.)
in association with Rosen Educational Services, LLC
29 East 21st Street, New York, NY 10010.

Distributed exclusively by Rosen Educational Services.
For a listing of additional Britannica Educational Publishing titles, call toll free (800) 237-9932.

First Edition

Britannica Educational Publishing
J.E. Luebering, Senior Manager
Adam Augustyn, Assistant Manager
Marilyn L. Barton: Senior Coordinator, Production Control
Steven Bosco: Director, Editorial Technologies
Lisa S. Braucher: Senior Producer and Data Editor
Yvette Charboneau: Senior Copy Editor
Kathy Nakamura: Manager, Media Acquisition
Jeff Wallenfeldt: Manager, Geography and History

Rosen Educational Services
Shalini Saxena: Editor
Nelson Sá: Art Director
Cindy Reiman: Photography Manager
Brian Garvey: Designer, Cover Design
Introduction by Jeff Wallenfeldt

Library of Congress Cataloging-in-Publication Data

U.S. imperialism and progressivism: 1896 to 1920/edited by Jeff Wallenfeldt.—1st ed.
     p. cm.—(Documenting America: the primary source documents of a nation)
Includes bibliographical references and index.
ISBN 978-1-61530-690-9 (library binding)
1. United States—Foreign relations—1865-1921. 2. United States—Territorial expansion.
3. Imperialism—History. 4. Progressivism (United States politics)—History. 5. United States—
Foreign relations—1865-1921—Sources. 6. United States—Territorial expansion—Sources.
7. Imperialism—History—Sources. 8. Progressivism (United States politics)—History—
Sources. I. Wallenfeldt, Jeffrey H. II. Title: US imperialism and progressivism.
E744.U137 2013
327.73009'034—dc23
                                                                    2011051612

Manufactured in the United States of America

On the cover: (main): The Spanish-American War launched the United States into international affairs, portending its later imperialist engagements. Theodore Roosevelt, shown here leading his Rough Riders during the war, was an instrumental figure for both imperialism and progressivism when he later took the office of president. *MPI/Archive Photos/Getty Images*

On the cover (document): The Roosevelt Corollary to the Monroe Doctrine. *Records of the U.S. House of Representatives, Record Group 233, Center for Legislative Archives, National Archives, Washington, D.C.*

On page viii: Theodore Roosevelt's stand against monopolies such as the Beef Trust represented his progressive sympathies and was the inspiration for this editorial cartoon. *Stock Montage/Archive Photos/Getty Images*

On pages 1, 10, 17, 24, 34, 42, 55: A map from the early 20th century showing the Panama Canal Zone. The Panama Canal helped strengthen American economic and national security and facilitated access to Pacific markets. *Buyenlarge/Archive Photos/Getty Images*

CONTENTS

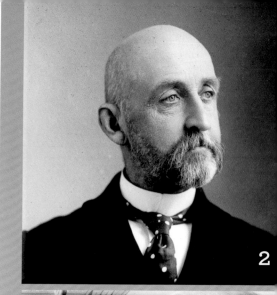

2

9

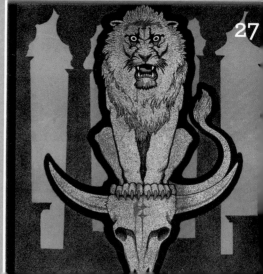

27

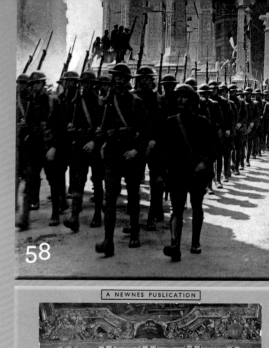

58

A NEWNES PUBLICATION

59

61

THESEUS ROOSEVELT AND THE MINOTAUR.

It's hard to imagine a pair of less likely fraternal twins than imperialism and progressivism, the defining concepts of American history for the period 1896–1920. Yet they were firmly harnessed not just in the arc of U.S. history but in the persons and policies of a pair of American presidents who indelibly stamped their influence on the period: Theodore Roosevelt and Woodrow Wilson. At first glance, Roosevelt and Wilson, like imperialism and progressivism, were a mismatched set—physically, temperamentally, and professionally; Roosevelt was stocky and robust, Wilson, tallish and gaunt. We picture Roosevelt on horseback, leading the charge of the Rough Riders up San Juan Hill in Cuba during the Spanish-American War. We see photos of him on hunting expeditions or surveying the wilderness he loved so dearly and did so much to preserve. Wilson, on the other hand, is ever the stately ivory-tower academic, the Princeton professor who put the ideas he explored in his scholarship to work in the living laboratory of the world at war and only occasionally donned a jaunty straw boater. The warrior and the priest, American historian John Milton Cooper called them, respectively, in his insightful study of the same name. But if Roosevelt and Wilson were as different as heads and tales, they were also two sides of the same coin—both progressives, and both, in their own way, imperialists. Both endeavoured to limit the laissez-faire autonomy and power of the corporation

in American life even as they sought to extend American political and economic influence throughout the world.

When he ran for the presidency in the 1912 election, Roosevelt was the ex-chief executive returning to the fray as a third-party (Bull Moose) candidate. He was disappointed in the direction the Republican Party had taken under Pres. William Howard Taft, Roosevelt's secretary of war and heir apparent, who in Roosevelt's mind had lost the political plot. And Roosevelt was disappointed by the Republicans, whose power brokers, at the end of the nomination process, had chosen Taft over the former president, even though Roosevelt had won such broad support within the party that Taft's own state, Ohio, backed him. Wilson's graceful rise from professor to university president to the governorship of New Jersey to nominee of the Democratic Party belied a cunning political gamesmanship that underlaid his image as a lofty idealist. Roosevelt and Wilson ran against the incumbent as "not Taft" candidates and against each other, seeking support across party lines for their own versions of the progressive agenda.

It was an exciting and important era in the history of the United States. How fascinating it would have been to be in Osawatomie, Kan., on Aug. 31, 1910, at the dedication of John Brown Battlefield. Here, Roosevelt took his first steps toward the 1912 presidential campaign with one of the most renowned speeches in American political history, in which he outlined the "New Nationalism" he envisioned as the progressive guiding principle for his country. Sitting in the gallery of the Senate chamber on Jan. 22, 1917, with the end of World War I imminent, how could one help but be inspired by Wilson's magnanimous plea for "Peace Without Victory" and his prescription for a world without "entangling alliances" in which states "plan for peace" and nations "accommodate their policy to it as they have planned for war and made ready for pitiless contest and rivalry." If only we could exploit the time-traveling technology of *Back to the Future* or persuade Doctor Who to take us with him as he journeys through time in his Police Box Tardis. In a way, though, we can—just not through the fanciful flight of science fiction. Reading history is time travel. And we are never so in the moment as when we engage with history's actors in their own words, when they are themselves deep in the moment, whether it be an impassioned speech, a provocative poem, carefully crafted legislation, a forceful essay, a fiery manifesto, or tactful but determined diplomacy. The primary sources in this volume vividly bring to life an America that is in the process of taking a starring role on the world's stage, with a supporting cast that includes not just Wilson and Roosevelt but Taft; "Fighting Bob" La Follette; "The Great Commoner," William Jennings Bryan; the suffragette's suffragette, Susan B. Anthony; Louis D. Brandeis; Jane Addams; and the Wobblies, among others. Their words are interwoven into a narrative history that describes the major events and themes of the era. Together that narrative and these primary sources are a time machine that makes it possible for readers to experience issues and events firsthand then pull back to draw conclusions with the benefit of reflection and hindsight. When the primary source documents are short, they are presented whole with the running text of the narrative; more often, excerpts are provided that give a flavour of the document, which is presented more fully in the Appendix. Specific introductions for each document provide additional context.

The imperialist impulse had already taken hold in the United States during the Spanish-American War when British author Rudyard Kipling challenged Americans to take up the "White Man's Burden" in 1899, inviting them to recognize their duty to bring what he saw as Anglo-Saxon enlightenment and guidance to peoples whose lands were often rich in natural resources. Newspapers had been quick to blame Spain for the sinking of the U.S. battleship *Maine* in Havana harbour in February 1898. War fever was stoked by the sensationalist jingoism of Joseph Pulitzer's *New York World* and William Randolph Hearst's *New York Journal* that became known as "yellow journalism" (because both rival newspapers ran a comic strip called "The Yellow Kid"). Many Americans shared the bellicose confidence expressed by journalist Albert Shaw, who believed "modern warfare has become a matter of machinery, and that the most highly developed mechanical and industrial nation will by virtue of such development be most formidable in war." Victory against Spain brought the United States an instant empire of possessions in the Caribbean and Pacific, including the Philippines, which diplomat Charles Denby was convinced the United States, "as conquerors," had the right to hold. He saw possession of them as a vital foothold in the Far East and rationalized American imperial expansion by writing, "Commerce, not politics, is king. The manufacturer and the merchant dictate to diplomacy and control elections." The Filipino revolutionaries who fought a courageous but ultimately futile insurrection against U.S. troops from 1899 to 1902 obviously did not agree. Neither did William Jennings Bryan, who staked much of his campaign as the Democratic Party's candidate for the presidency in 1900 on opposition to imperialism. "We cannot repudiate the principle of self-government in the Philippines without weakening that principle here [in the United States]," Bryan said. He lost the argument and the election.

In attempting to increase its presence in East Asia, the United States came up against the interests of the German and Russian empires, which had already established "spheres of influence" in China. In 1899 U.S. Secretary of State John Hay pushed those countries to adopt an "Open Door Policy" that would buttress Chinese independence while "insuring the benefits of equality of treatment of all foreign trade throughout China." The

growing American interest in the Pacific at the turn of the century also contributed to expanded U.S. involvement in Central America, where frustrated French and British efforts to build a canal connecting the Atlantic and Pacific were replaced by an American project that proved successful, but only after Panama (with outside help) had obtained its independence from Colombia, which had been reluctant to allow the United States to construct the Panama Canal. The intensification of U.S. intervention in the region was announced by Pres. Theodore Roosevelt in his Corollary to Monroe Doctrine of 1905, in which he declared that the United States would "help upward toward peace and order those of our sister republics which need such help." Who actually benefited from repeated U.S. intervention in the internal affairs of those Latin American countries remains a matter of interpretation.

On the U.S. home front, working-class Americans, both urban and rural, struggled to make ends meet in a society dominated by corporations that were largely given a free hand. The Progressive movement that rose to fight for the rights of these people had its origins in the Granger and Populist movements of the 19th century. One of its guiding lights, settlement-house founder Jane Addams, believed that the relationship between employer and employee had to be a democratic one aimed at the attainment of "social morality." For Robert M. La Follette, the governor of

Wisconsin, whom journalist Amos P. Wilder described as grappling with "the modern lions that guard the portals where privilege is entrenched," the principle of "popular control" was paramount. As reflected in their 1905 manifesto, the Industrial Workers of the World, better known as the Wobblies, sought to bring labourers together in "one great industrial union embracing all industries, providing for craft autonomy locally, industrial autonomy internationally, and working-class unity generally." In the White House, Roosevelt, who used the presidency as a "bully pulpit" to advance progressive causes, attempted to breathe ferocious new life into the Sherman Anti-Trust Act and to extend the authority of the Interstate Commerce Commission. The progressive momentum slowed, however, when Taft, who succeeded Roosevelt as president, proved to be much less of a progressive than had been thought. Indeed, he earned the enmity of progressives when he not only signed a bill that raised the tariff but praised it as "the best tariff bill that the Republican Party ever passed."

When Wilson triumphed in the 1912 election, progressivism again had a champion in the White House. In his first inaugural address, Wilson emphasized that government had "too often been made use of for private and selfish purposes" and that "those who used it had forgotten the people." In criticizing the heedless rush to succeed, he said that Americans had not "studied and perfected

the means by which government may be put at the service of humanity." Wilson pushed through tax reform and oversaw the formation of the Federal Reserve and the Federal Commerce Commission. One of his closest advisers was future Supreme Court justice Louis D. Brandeis, who inveighed against "the money trust."

A true believer in democratic government, Wilson was outraged by the autocratic Victoriano Huerta's assumption of power in Mexico in 1913, and he took the hardest of lines when U.S. sailors were briefly incarcerated in Tampico, Mex., in 1914. Later that year, Wilson authorized U.S. forces to seize the Mexican port of Veracruz in an attempt to help bring about Huerta's downfall. Events drew Wilson and the United States deeper into international affairs, especially with the onset of World War I. Wilson, who said "there is such a thing as a man being too proud to fight," aggressively pursued neutrality, even after American lives began to be lost as the result of German submarine warfare against ships traveling to and from Britain. When 128 Americans died in the sinking of the British ship *Lusitania* in 1915, longtime pacifist Bryan, then serving as Wilson's secretary of state, took the Imperial German government to task, requesting tactfully but forcefully that it "correct the unfortunate impressions which have been created and vindicate once more the position of that government with regard to the sacred freedom of the seas." As American involvement in the war began to appear imminent, "preparedness advocate" Maj. Gen. Leonard Wood pointed to the need for Americans to get beyond "the curious Anglo-Saxon prejudice against a large standing army and the feeling that it is always a menace to civil liberty" to arrive at a "condition of thorough preparedness...without creating a condition of militarism."

Once U.S. troops became involved, making the journey across the Atlantic to the strains of George M. Cohan's "Over There," the country united behind the war effort, though support for the war was far from universal, as can be seen in what historian Charles A. Beard saw as Columbia's University's intolerance of antiwar dissent among its faculty. American involvement on the Allied side had much to do with determining the outcome of the war, and Wilson sought to play a major role in shaping the peace and the postwar world to come. With "Peace without Victory" as his starting point, he fashioned the "Fourteen Points" as a blueprint for a better world, one that by 1920 would finally come to include the franchise for American women, guaranteed by the Nineteenth Amendment, the culmination of the long struggle of women's rights activists such as Susan B. Anthony. The fullness of Wilson's vision would never come to pass, however. Most poignantly, the United States would never join the League of Nations, the international body Wilson had conceived as the guarantor of world peace through rational discussion and diplomacy. American membership was politically torpedoed by Republican senators, led by Henry Cabot Lodge, who sought either to reject the treaty or to attach reservations that would gravely limit America's commitments to the League. That failure, along with the stroke that would largely incapacitate Wilson for the remainder of his presidency, effectively marked the end of the Progressive era.

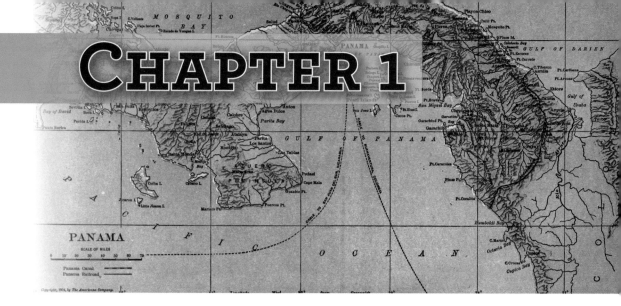

CHAPTER 1

AMERICAN
IMPERIALISM

Militarily speaking, the Spanish-American War of 1898 was so brief and relatively bloodless as to have been a mere passing episode in the history of modern warfare. Its political and diplomatic consequences, however, were enormous: it catapulted the United States into the arena of world politics and set it, at least briefly, on the new road of imperialism. To be sure, specific events drove the United States to hostilities in 1898; but the stage had already been set by profound changes in thought about the country's mission and its destiny.

Before the 1890s, roughly speaking, most Americans had adhered stubbornly to the belief, as old as the Revolution itself, that their country should remain aloof from European affairs and offer an example of democracy and peace to the rest of the world; but slowly in the 1880s, and more rapidly in the 1890s, new currents of thought eroded this historic conviction. The United States had become a great power by virtue of its prodigious economic growth since the Civil War; numerous publicists said that it ought to begin to act like one. Propagandists of sea power, above all, Capt. Alfred T. Mahan,

Alfred T. Mahan. Buyenlarge/Archive Photos/Getty Images

argued that future national security and greatness depended upon a large navy supported by bases throughout the world. After the disappearance of the American frontier in 1890, the conviction grew that the United States would have to find new outlets for an ever-increasing population and agricultural and industrial production; this belief was particularly rife among farmers in dire distress in the 1890s. Social Darwinists said that the world is a jungle, with international rivalries inevitable, and that only strong countries could survive. Added to these arguments were those of idealists and religious leaders that Americans had a duty to "take up the white man's burden" and to carry their assertedly superior

Document: Rudyard Kipling: "The White Man's Burden" (1899)

British author Rudyard Kipling had seen enough of his own country's far-flung colonial ventures to be able to suggest to Americans what the real meaning of their new imperialism might be. While the debate over the Philippines was raging, Kipling addressed to Americans a poem entitled "The White Man's Burden," which, despite its ironic tone, struck a note of nobility that was seized upon by expansionists. It was the title rather than the content of the poem that provided a catchphrase for imperialists, and the paternalistic poem, which was first published in McClure's *magazine and widely reprinted throughout the country within a week, did much to bolster the expansionist cause.*

McClure's, *February 1899.*

THE WHITE MAN'S BURDEN

Take up the white man's burden —
Send forth the best ye breed —
Go, bind your sons to exile
To serve your captives' need;
To wait, in heavy harness,
On fluttered folk and wild —
Your new-caught sullen peoples,
Half devil and half child.

Take up the white man's burden —
In patience to abide,
To veil the threat of terror
And check the show of pride;
By open speech and simple,
A hundred times made plain,
To seek another's profit
And work another's gain.

Take up the white man's burden —
The savage wars of peace —
Fill full the mouth of famine,
And bid the sickness cease;
And when your goal is nearest
(The end for others sought)
Watch sloth and heathen folly
Bring all your hope to nought.

Take up the white man's burden —
No iron rule of kings,
But toil of serf and sweeper —
The tale of common things.
The ports ye shall not enter,
The roads ye shall not tread,
Go, make them with your living
And mark them with your dead.

Take up the white man's burden,
And reap his old reward —
The blame of those ye better
The hate of those ye guard —
The cry of hosts ye humor
(Ah, slowly!) toward the light:
"Why brought ye us from bondage,
Our loved Egyptian night?"

Take up the white man's burden —
Ye dare not stoop to less —
Nor call too loud on Freedom
To cloak your weariness.
By all ye will or whisper,
By all ye leave or do,
The silent sullen peoples
Shall weigh your God and you.

Take up the white man's burden!
Have done with childish days —
The lightly proffered laurel,
The easy ungrudged praise:
Comes now, to search your manhood
Through all the thankless years,
Cold, edged with dear-bought wisdom,
The judgment of your peers.

culture and the blessings of Christianity to the backward peoples of the world.

THE SPANISH-AMERICAN WAR

It was against this background that the events of 1898 propelled the United States along the road to war and empire. Cuban rebels had begun a violent revolution against Spanish rule in 1895, set off by a depression caused by a decline in U.S. sugar purchases from Cuba. Rebel violence led progressively to more repressive Spanish countermeasures. Cuban refugees in the United States spread exaggerated tales of Spanish atrocities, and these and numerous others were reprinted widely (particularly by William Randolph Hearst's New York *American* and Joseph Pulitzer's New York *World*, then engaged in a fierce battle for circulation). Pres. Grover Cleveland resisted the rising public demand for intervention, but by early 1898 the pressure, then on his successor, William McKinley, was too great to be defied. When an explosion—caused by a submarine mine, according to a U.S. naval court of inquiry—sank the USS *Maine* with large loss of life in Havana harbour on Feb. 15, 1898, events moved beyond the president's control.

An illustration showing the remains of the USS Maine *in Havana harbour in Cuba.* Library of Congress Prints and Photographs Division

Document: Albert Shaw: The Blowing up of the *Maine* (1898)

After the United States battleship Maine was blown up in Havana harbour on Feb. 15, 1898, the American Court of Inquiry published the results of its investigation into the disaster. The court did not assign responsibility but simply concluded that a submarine mine was the cause of the explosion. Whether the explosion was produced by Cuban rebels desiring American intervention, or by irresponsible Spanish loyalists, or simply by an accident, will never be known. But to the newspapers in the United States that wanted war with Spain, the guilt was clear. The newspaper headlines of influential publisher William Randolph Hearst read: "Maine Was Destroyed By Treachery!" and "The Whole Country Thrills With War Fever!" Albert Shaw, editorializing in the Review of Reviews *in April, shared the popular view and expressed great confidence in the war-making potential of the United States.*

The weeks that have elapsed since that fatal event of February 15th have been making history in a manner highly creditable to the American government and to our citizenship. Captain Sigsbee, the commander of the *Maine*, had promptly telegraphed his desire that judgment should be suspended until investigation had been made. The investigation was set on foot at once, and 75 million Americans have accordingly suspended judgment in the face of a great provocation. For it must be remembered that to suppose the destruction of the *Maine* an ordinary accident and not due to any external agency or hostile intent was, under all the circumstances, to set completely at defiance the law of probabilities.

It is not true that battleships are in the habit of blowing themselves up. When all the environing facts were taken into consideration, it was just about as probable that the *Maine* had been blown up by spontaneous combustion or by some accident in which no hostile motive was concerned, as that the reported assassination of President Barrios of Guatemala, a few days previously, had really been a suicide....

Though Spain was willing to make large concessions to avoid war, it adamantly resisted what had become the minimum public and official U.S. demand—Spanish withdrawal from Cuba and recognition of the island's independence. Hence Congress in mid-April authorized McKinley to use the armed forces to expel the Spanish from Cuba.

For Americans it was, as Secretary of State John Hay put it in a letter to Theodore Roosevelt, "a splendid little war." An American expeditionary force, after quickly overcoming the Spaniards in Cuba, turned against Spain's last island in the Caribbean, Puerto Rico. Meanwhile, on May 1, 1898, the American commodore George Dewey, with his Asiatic squadron, destroyed a decrepit Spanish flotilla in the harbour of Manila in the Philippines.

The fighting was over by August 12, when the United States and Spain signed a preliminary peace treaty in Washington, D.C. Negotiators met in Paris in October to draw up a definitive agreement. Spain

Document: Charles Denby: The Evident Fitness of Keeping the Philippines (1898)

Charles Denby, the former U.S. minister to China, had long been an ardent supporter of American expansion into East Asia. "The Pacific Ocean," he had written to the administration prior to the Spanish-American War of 1898, "is destined to bear on its bosom a larger commerce than the Atlantic." Denby was delighted to become a member of Pres. William McKinley's commission to study the Philippines after the islands had been acquired as a result of the peace negotiations with Spain. In the following article, published in November 1898, Denby gave further reasons why the United States should retain the islands.

Dewey's victory has changed our attitude before the world. We took no part in international questions. We had no standing in the councils of the nations. We were a *quantité négligeable*. So far did the idea that we ought to take no part in foreign questions extend that some of my colleagues at Peking, when I undertook to make peace for China and Japan, deprecated any intervention whatever of the United States in the affairs of the Far East!

The position of absolute indifference to what is happening in the world is difficult of maintenance; and when it is maintained it is humiliating....

I recognize the existence of a national sentiment in accordance with the supposed teaching of Washington's Farewell Address, which is against the acquisition of foreign territory; but the world has moved and circumstances are changed. We have become a great people. We have a great commerce to take care of. We have to compete with the commercial nations of the world in far-distant markets. Commerce, not politics, is king. The manufacturer and the merchant dictate to diplomacy and control elections. The art of arts is the extension of commercial relations—in plain language, the selling of native products and manufactured goods....

recognized the independence of Cuba and ceded Puerto Rico and Guam to the United States, but the disposition of the Philippines was another matter. Business interests in the United States, which had been noticeably cool about a war over Cuba, demanded the acquisition of the entire Philippine archipelago in the hope that Manila would become the entrepôt for a great Far Eastern trade; chauvinists

William Jennings Bryan. Library of Congress Prints and Photographs Division

Document: William Jennings Bryan: The Paralyzing Influence of Imperialism (1900)

In his second campaign for the presidency in 1900, William Jennings Bryan focused his criticism on the Republican administration's imperialistic policy. An avowed pacifist, Bryan had been against the Spanish-American War of 1898 but had supported the peace treaty; he had hoped that a speedy conclusion to the war would provide the Filipinos with their independence. In his acceptance speech as the nominee of the Democratic Party at its convention at Military Park, Indianapolis, Ind., on Aug. 8, 1900, part of which is reprinted here, Bryan outlined what his objections to imperialism were and what he, as president, would do instead. In Bryan's opinion, Rudyard Kipling's famous "white man's burden," which was taken up during the Spanish-American War, had to be put down; Bryan hoped to satisfy one anti-imperialistic newspaper, which had asked: "Now will you kindly tell us, Rudyard,/How we may put it down?".

If it is right for the United States to hold the Philippine Islands permanently and imitate European empires in the government of colonies, the Republican Party ought to state its position and defend it, but it must expect the subject races to protest against such a policy and to resist to the extent of their ability.

The Filipinos do not need any encouragement from Americans now living. Our whole history has been an encouragement, not only to the Filipinos but to all who are denied a voice in their own government. If the Republicans are prepared to censure all who have used language calculated to make the Filipinos hate foreign domination, let them condemn the speech of Patrick Henry. When he uttered that passionate appeal, "Give me liberty or give me death," he expressed a sentiment which still echoes in the hearts of men.

Let them censure Jefferson; of all the statesmen of history none have used words so offensive to those who would hold their fellows in political bondage. Let them censure Washington, who declared that the colonists must choose between liberty and slavery. Or, if the statute of limitations has run against the sins of Henry and Jefferson and Washington, let them censure Lincoln, whose Gettysburg speech will be quoted in defense of popular government when the present advocates of force and conquest are forgotten....

declaimed against lowering the flag under Spanish pressure. Concluding that he had no alternative, McKinley forced the Spanish to "sell" the Philippines to the United States for $20,000,000.

But a strong reaction in the United States against acquisition of the Philippines had already set in by the time the Treaty of Paris was signed on Dec. 10, 1898; and anti-imperialists declared that the control and governance of distant alien peoples violated all American traditions of self-determination and would even threaten the very fabric of the republic. Though there were more than enough votes in the Senate to defeat the treaty, that body gave its consent to ratification largely because William Jennings

A campaign poster for William McKinley, who twice defeated Democratic candidate William Jennings Bryan in the race for the presidency, once in 1896, and again in 1900. Buyenlarge/Archive Photos/Getty Images

Bryan, the Democratic leader, wanted Democrats to approve the treaty and then make imperialism the chief issue of the 1900 presidential campaign.

THE NEW AMERICAN EMPIRE

McKinley easily defeated Bryan in 1900. The victory, however, was hardly a mandate for imperialism, and, as events were soon to disclose, the American people were perhaps the most reluctant imperialists in history. No sooner had they acquired an overseas empire than they set in motion the process of its dissolution or transformation.

By the so-called Teller Amendment to the war resolution, Congress had declared that the United States would not annex Cuba. This pledge was kept, although Cuba was forced in 1903 to sign a treaty making it virtually a protectorate of the United States. The Hawaiian Islands, annexed by Congress on July 7, 1898, were made a territory in 1900 and were hence, technically, only briefly part of the American empire. Puerto Rico was given limited self-government in 1900; the Jones Act of 1917 conferred full territorial status on the island, gave U.S. citizenship to its inhabitants, and limited its self-government only by the veto of a governor appointed by the president of the United States. Establishing any kind of government in the Philippines was much more difficult because a large band of Filipinos resisted American rule as bravely as they had fought the Spanish. The Philippine insurrection was over by 1901, however, and the Philippine Government Act of 1902 inaugurated the beginning of partial self-government, which was transformed into almost complete home rule by the Jones Act of 1916.

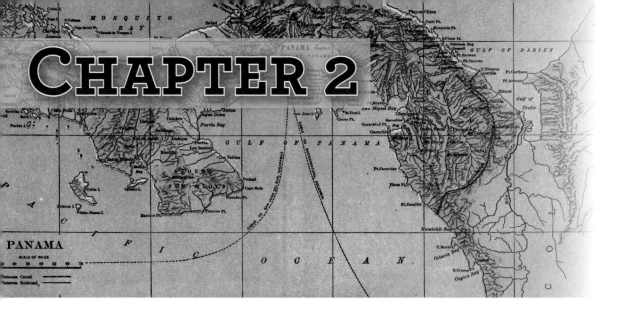

CHAPTER 2

PANAMA

UNLOCKING THE PACIFIC

Although Americans were reluctant imperialists, the United States was an important Pacific power after 1898, and American businessmen had inflated ambitions to tap what they thought was the huge Chinese market. The continued growth of the U.S. Navy after the Spanish-American War fueled the fire of these aspirations. Reflective of the Navy's expansion in the early 20th century was the development of a first-class naval base at Pearl Harbor, Hawaii, the site of an historic East-West collision later in the century.

THE OPEN DOOR IN THE FAR EAST

The doors to the Chinese market were being rapidly closed in the 1890s, however, as Britain, France, Russia, and Japan carved out large so-called spheres of influence all the way from Manchuria to southern China. With Britain's encouragement, on Sept. 6, 1899, Secretary of State John Hay addressed the first so-called Open Door note to the powers with interests in China; it asked them to accord equal trade and investment opportunities to all nationals in their spheres of interest and leased territories.

Document: John Hay: The Open Door Policy (1899)

In 1899 trade with China amounted to only about 2 percent of the total U.S. trade. Nevertheless, the American government was concerned that China's independence be preserved in the hope that trade might increase. Great Britain—which had a greater stake in China and stood to gain a great deal from equal trade opportunities—shared this concern and prodded the United States, behind the scenes, into diplomatic action. The provisions of the "Open Door Policy" articulated by U.S. Secretary of State Hay in the "circular letter" sent to Germany, Russia, and Britain on Sept. 6, 1899, were rather narrow, but his letter (printed here) was followed up the next year by a broader guarantee of China's territorial integrity.

At the time when the government of the United States was informed by that of Germany that it had leased from His Majesty the Emperor of China the port of Kiaochao and the adjacent territory in the province of Shantung, assurances were given to the ambassador of the United States at Berlin by the Imperial German minister for foreign affairs that the rights and privileges insured by treaties with China to citizens of the United States would not thereby suffer or be in anywise impaired within the area over which Germany had thus obtained control.

More recently, however, the British government recognized by a formal agreement with Germany the exclusive right of the latter country to enjoy in said leased area and the contiguous "sphere of influence or interest" certain privileges, more especially those relating to railroads and mining enterprises; but, as the exact nature and extent of the rights thus recognized have not been clearly defined, it is possible that serious conflicts of interest may at any time arise, not only between British and German subjects within said area but that the interests of our citizens may also be jeopardized thereby.

Earnestly desirous to remove any cause of irritation and to insure at the same time to the commerce of all nations in China the undoubted benefits which should accrue from a formal recognition by the various powers claiming "spheres of interest" that they shall enjoy perfect equality of treatment for their commerce and navigation within such "spheres," the government of the United States would be pleased to see His German Majesty's government give formal assurances and lend its cooperation in securing like assurances from the other interested powers that each within its respective sphere of whatever influence....

With considerable bravado, Hay announced that all the powers had agreed to respect the Open Door, even though the Russians had declined to give any pledges. On July 3, 1900, after the Boxer Rebellion—an uprising in China against foreign influence—Hay circulated a second Open Door note announcing that it was American policy to preserve Chinese territorial and political integrity.

Such pronouncements had little effect because the United States was not prepared to support the Open Door policy with force; successive administrations to the 1940s, however, considered it the cornerstone of their Far Eastern policy. Pres.

John Hay. Hulton Archive/Getty Images

BUILDING THE PANAMA CANAL AND AMERICAN DOMINATION IN THE CARIBBEAN

Strategic necessity and the desire of Eastern businessmen to have easy access to Pacific markets combined in the late 1890s to convince the president, Congress, and a vast majority of Americans that an isthmian canal linking the Atlantic and Pacific oceans was vital to national security and prosperity. In the Hay–Pauncefote Treaty of 1901, the British government gave up the rights to joint construction with the United States that it had gained under the Clayton–Bulwer Treaty of 1850. A French company, which had tried unsuccessfully to dig a canal across the Isthmus of Panama, was eager to sell its right-of-way to the United States. Thus, the only obstacle to the project was the government of Colombia, which owned Panama. When Colombia was slow to cooperate, Roosevelt, in 1903, covertly supported a Panamanian revolution engineered by officials of the French company. A treaty was quickly negotiated between the United States and the new Republic of Panama; construction began, and the canal was opened to shipping on Aug. 15, 1914.

Concern over what Americans regarded increasingly as their "lifeline" increased in proportion to progress in the construction of the canal. An early manifestation of that concern came in 1902–03, when Britain, Germany, and Italy blockaded

Theodore Roosevelt reluctantly mediated the Russo-Japanese War in 1905 in part to protect the Open Door as well as to maintain a balance of power in the Far East. When Japan attempted in 1915 to force a virtual protectorate on China, Pres. Woodrow Wilson intervened sternly and in some measure successfully to protect Chinese independence. Victory for American policy seemed to come with the Nine-Power Treaty of Washington of 1922, when all countries with interests in China promised to respect the Open Door.

American construction of the Panama Canal, shown here, began in 1904 and continued for a number of years. The canal was open for use in 1914. Hulton Archive/Getty Images

Venezuela to force the payment of debts, and particularly when the Germans bombarded and destroyed a Venezuelan town. So agitated was American opinion that Roosevelt used a veiled threat to force Germany to accept arbitration of the debt question by the Hague Court. When the Dominican Republic defaulted on its foreign debt to several European countries in 1904, Roosevelt quickly established an American receivership of the Dominican customs in order to collect the revenues to meet the country's debt payments. Moreover, in his annual message to Congress of 1904, the president announced a new Latin-American policy, soon called the Roosevelt Corollary to the Monroe Doctrine—because the Monroe Doctrine forbade European use of force in the New World, the United States would itself take whatever action necessary to guarantee that Latin-American states gave no cause for such European intervention. It was, in fact, a considerable extension of the Monroe Doctrine, not a correct historical interpretation of it, but it remained

THE PRESIDENT IS NOW "SPEAKING GENTLY."

Newspapers and editorial cartoons of the day often referenced Theodore Roosevelt's fondness for the West African saying "Speak softly and carry a big stick; you will go far." This cartoon refers to Roosevelt's usage of that policy in mediating the settlement of the Russo-Japanese War (1904-05). Library of Congress Prints and Photographs Division

the cornerstone of American policy in the Caribbean at least until 1928.

Actually, Roosevelt was reluctant to interfere in the domestic affairs of neighbouring states; his one significant intervention after 1904—the administration of the Cuban government from 1906 to 1909—was undertaken in order to prevent civil war and at the insistence of Cuban authorities. Roosevelt's successor as president, however, William Howard Taft, had more ambitious plans to guarantee American hegemony in the approaches to the Panama Canal. Adopting a policy called Dollar Diplomacy, Taft hoped to persuade American private bankers to displace European creditors in the Caribbean area and thereby to increase American influence and encourage stability in countries prone to revolution. Dollar Diplomacy was a total failure; its one result was to involve the United States in a civil war in Nicaragua with the effect of perpetuating a reactionary and unpopular regime. (Similar initiatives by the Taft administration in the Far East—most notably a plan for the internationalization of the railroads of Manchuria—also failed.)

Document: Theodore Roosevelt: Corollary to the Monroe Doctrine (1905)

The blockade in 1902 off the coast of Venezuela by creditor countries Germany, Italy, and England concerned Pres. Theodore Roosevelt. Anxious about the presence of Europeans in the vicinity of the uncompleted Panama Canal, Roosevelt made a show of naval force and urged U.S. mediation. Two years later, when European powers threatened forcibly to collect debts owed them by the Dominican Republic, the United States again intervened to make the collection. In his annual messages to Congress in 1904 and 1905, Roosevelt formulated his "corollary" to the Monroe Doctrine, urging a new role for the United States—that of international policeman for the Western Hemisphere. In the message of 1905, which is reprinted here in part, he spelled out in detail how the role was to be conceived.

One of the most effective instruments for peace is the Monroe Doctrine as it has been and is being gradually developed by this nation and accepted by other nations. No other policy could have been as efficient in promoting peace in the Western Hemisphere and in giving to each nation thereon the chance to develop along its own lines. If we had refused to apply the doctrine to changing conditions, it would now be completely outworn, would not meet any of the needs of the present day, and, indeed, would probably by this time have sunk into complete oblivion.

It is useful at home and is meeting with recognition abroad because we have adapted our application of it to meet the growing and changing needs of the Hemisphere. When we announce a policy such as the Monroe Doctrine, we thereby commit ourselves to the consequences of the policy, and those consequences from time to time alter. It is out of the question to claim a right and yet shirk the responsibility for its exercise. Not only we but all American republics who are benefited by the existence of the doctrine must recognize the obligations each nation is under as regards foreign peoples, no less than its duty to insist upon its own rights....

William Howard Taft speaking in Springfield, Mass. Library of Congress Prints and Photographs Division

The accession of Woodrow Wilson in 1913 seemed to augur the beginning of a new era in Latin-American relations; the new president and his secretary of state, William Jennings Bryan, were idealists who had strongly condemned interventions and Dollar Diplomacy. But, although Wilson did negotiate a treaty with Colombia to make reparation for U.S. complicity in the Panamanian revolution, it was defeated by the Senate. Wilson also tried hard to promote a Pan-American nonaggression pact, but it foundered on the opposition of Chile, which had a long-standing border dispute with Peru.

When crises threatened the domestic stability of the Caribbean area,

however, Wilson revealed that he was just as determined to protect American security as Roosevelt and Taft had been and that he was perhaps even more willing to use force. Frequent revolutions and the fear of European intervention led Wilson to impose a protectorate and a puppet government upon Haiti in 1915 and a military occupation of the Dominican Republic in 1916. He concluded a treaty with Nicaragua making that country a protectorate of the United States. Moreover, he purchased the Danish Virgin Islands in 1916 at the inflated price of $25,000,000 in order to prevent their possible transfer from Denmark to Germany.

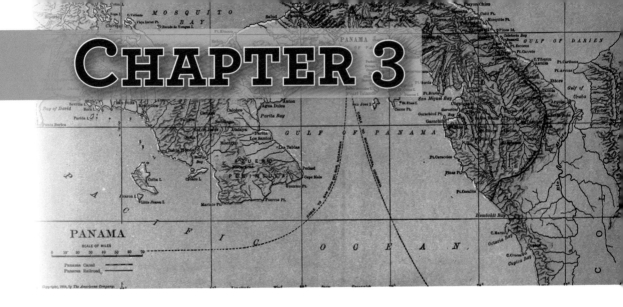

CHAPTER 3

THE PROGRESSIVE MOVEMENT

The inauguration of President McKinley in 1897 had seemed to mark the end of an era of domestic turmoil and the beginning of a new period of unparalleled tranquility. Prosperity was returning after the devastating panic of 1893. The agrarian uprising led by Bryan in the election of 1896 had been turned back, and the national government was securely in the hands of friends of big business. The Dingley Tariff Act of 1897 greatly increased tariff rates; the Gold Standard Act of 1897 dashed the hopes of advocates of the free coinage of silver; and McKinley did nothing to stop a series of industrial combinations in defiance of the Sherman Anti-Trust Act.

William McKinley making his inaugural address on March 4, 1897. Outgoing president Grover Cleveland looks on. Library of Congress Prints and Photographs Division

THE ORIGINS OF PROGRESSIVISM

Never were superficial signs more deceiving. Actually, the United States already was in the first stages of what historians came to call the Progressive movement. Generally speaking, progressivism was the response of various groups to problems raised by the rapid industrialization and urbanization that followed the Civil War. These problems included the spread of slums and poverty; the exploitation of labour; the breakdown of democratic government in the cities and states caused by the emergence of political organizations, or machines, allied with business interests; and a rapid movement toward financial and industrial concentration. Many Americans feared that their historic traditions of responsible democratic government and free economic opportunity for all were being destroyed by gigantic combinations of economic and political power.

Progressive movements evolved in part in response to the conditions of increasingly prevalent slums, such as this one in New York City, photographed by muckracking journalist-photographer Jacob A. Riis, remembered for his book How the Other Half Lives. *Jacob A. Riis/Hulton Archive/ Getty Images*

Actually there was not, either in the 1890s or later, any single Progressive movement. The numerous movements for reform on the local, state, and national levels were too diverse, and sometimes too mutually antagonistic, ever to coalesce into a national crusade. But they were generally motivated by common assumptions and goals—e.g., the repudiation of individualism and laissez-faire, concern for the underprivileged and downtrodden, the control of government by the rank and file, and the enlargement of governmental power in order to bring

Jane Addams sitting with a young girl in the Hull House nursery. Women and children were among those who benefitted from services provided by Hull House. Wallace Kirkland/Time & Life Pictures/Getty Images

industry and finance under a measure of popular control.

The origins of progressivism were as complex and are as difficult to describe as the movement itself. In the vanguard were various agrarian crusaders, such as the Grangers and the Populists and Democrats under Bryan, with their demands for stringent railroad regulation and national control of banks and the money supply. At the same time a new generation of economists, sociologists, and political scientists was undermining the philosophical foundations of the laissez-faire state and constructing a new ideology to justify democratic collectivism, while a new school of social workers was establishing settlement houses and going into the slums to discover the extent of human degradation.

The settlement movement had begun with the founding of Toynbee Hall in the Whitechapel industrial district in London in 1884. The movement spread to the United States when Charles B. Stover and an American lecturer at the West London Ethical Society, Stanton Coit, an early visitor to Toynbee Hall, established Neighborhood Guild, now University Settlement, on the Lower East Side of New York City, in 1886. In 1889 Jane Addams bought a residence on Chicago's West Side that came to be known as Hull House. In the same year the educator Jane E. Robbins and Jean Fine (Mrs. Charles B. Spahr) opened the College Settlement, in New York City. Two years later Robert A. Woods, another resident of Toynbee Hall, and William J. Tucker established

Jane Addams

Social reformer and pacifist Jane Addams is best known as the founder of Hull House. She graduated from Rockford Female Seminary in Illinois in 1881 and was granted a degree the following year when the institution became Rockford College. Following the death of her father in 1881, her own health problems, and an unhappy year at the Woman's Medical College, Philadelphia, she was an invalid for two years. During neither subsequent travel in Europe in 1883–85 nor her stay in Baltimore, Md., in 1885–87 did she find a vocation.

In 1887–88 Addams returned to Europe with a Rockford classmate, Ellen Gates Starr. On a visit to Toynbee Hall Addams's vague leanings toward reform work crystallized. Upon returning to the United States, she and Starr determined to create something like Toynbee Hall. In a working-class immigrant district in Chicago, they acquired a large vacant residence built by Charles Hull in 1856, and, calling it Hull House, they moved into it on Sept. 18, 1889. Eventually the settlement included 13 buildings and a playground, as well as a camp near Lake Geneva, Wis. Many prominent social workers and reformers—Julia Lathrop, Florence Kelley, and Grace and Edith Abbott—came to live at Hull House, as did others who continued to make their living in business or the arts while helping Addams in settlement activities.

Among the facilities at Hull House were a day nursery, a gymnasium, a community kitchen, and a boarding club for working girls. Hull House offered college-level courses in various subjects, furnished training in art, music, and crafts such as bookbinding, and sponsored one of the earliest little-theatre groups, the Hull House Players. In addition to making available services and cultural opportunities for the largely immigrant population of the neighbourhood, Hull House afforded an opportunity for young social workers to acquire training.

Addams worked with labour as well as other reform groups toward goals including the first juvenile-court law, tenement-house regulation, an eight-hour working day for women, factory inspection, and workers' compensation. She strove in addition for justice for immigrants and blacks, advocated research aimed at determining the causes of poverty and crime, and supported woman suffrage. In 1910 she became the first woman president of the National Conference of Social Work, and in 1912 she played an active part in the Progressive Party's presidential campaign for Theodore Roosevelt. At The Hague in 1915 she served as chairman of the International Congress of Women, following which was established the Women's International League for Peace and Freedom. She was also involved in the founding of the American Civil Liberties Union in 1920. In 1931 she was a cowinner (with Nicholas Murray Butler) of the Nobel Prize for Peace.

The establishment of the Chicago campus of the University of Illinois in 1963 forced the Hull House Association to relocate its headquarters. The majority of its original buildings were demolished, but the Hull residence itself was preserved as a monument to Jane Addams.

Among Addams's books are Democracy and Social Ethics *(1902),* Newer Ideals of Peace *(1907),* Twenty Years at Hull-House *(1910), and* The Second Twenty Years at Hull-House *(1930).*

Andover House, later called South End House, in Boston.

Allied with the progressive academics, agrarian crusaders, and social workers was a growing body of ministers, priests, and rabbis—proponents of what was called the social Gospel—who struggled to arouse the social concerns and consciences of their parishioners. Finally, journalists called "muckrakers" probed into all the dark corners of American life and carried their message of reform through mass-circulation newspapers and magazines.

Two specific catalytic agents set off the Progressive movement—the agrarian depression of the early 1890s and the financial and industrial depression that began in 1893. Low prices drove farmers by the hundreds of thousands into the People's Party of 1892. Widespread suffering in the cities beginning in 1893 caused a breakdown of many social services and, for the increasing number of urban middle-class Americans, dramatized the gross inefficiency of most municipal governments.

URBAN REFORMS

A movement already begun, to wrest control of city governments from corrupt

Document: Jane Addams: Industrial Amelioration and Social Ethics (1902)

Working at Hull House among immigrants gave Addams intimate knowledge of the harsh realities of life in an industrial world. She witnessed the bewilderment of new arrivals who did not know how to find a job or even how to go about training for one, and who therefore often stumbled irretrievably in their first attempts at a new life. Her experiences led her to agitate for social reform, and her book Democracy and Social Ethics, *from which the following selection is taken, discussed the kind of social and moral changes that would have to occur before America could realize its promises.*

The man who disassociates his ambition, however disinterested, from the cooperation of his fellows, always takes [the] risk of ultimate failure. He does not take advantage of the great conserver and guarantee of his own permanent success which associated efforts afford. Genuine experiments toward higher social conditions must have a more democratic faith and practice than those which underlie private venture. Public parks and improvements, intended for the common use, are after all only safe in the hands of the public itself; and associated effort toward social progress, although much more awkward and stumbling than that same effort managed by a capable individual, does yet enlist deeper forces and evoke higher social capacities.

The successful businessman who is also the philanthropist is in more than the usual danger of getting widely separated from his employees. The men already have the American veneration for wealth and successful business capacity, and, added to this, they are dazzled by his good works. The workmen have the same kindly impulses as he, but while they organize their charity into mutual benefit associations and distribute their money in small amounts in relief for the widows and insurance for the injured, the employer may build model towns, erect college buildings, which are tangible and enduring, and thereby display his goodness in concentrated form....

political machines, was given tremendous impetus by the panic of 1893. The National Municipal League, organized in 1894, united various city reform groups throughout the country; corrupt local governments were overthrown in such cities as New York in 1894, Baltimore in 1895, and Chicago in 1896–97. And so it went all over the country well into the 20th century.

Despite initial differences among urban reformers, by the early 1900s the vast majority of them were fighting for and winning many of the same objectives—more equitable taxation of railroad and corporate property, tenement house reform, better schools, and expanded social services for the poor. Even big-city machines like Tammany Hall became increasingly sensitive to the social and economic needs of their constituents. Reformers also devised new forms of city government to replace the old mayor–city-council arrangement that had proved to be so susceptible to corrupt influences. One was the commission form, which vested all responsibility in a small group of commissioners, each responsible for a single department; another was the city-manager form, which provided administration by a professionally trained expert, responsible to a popularly elected council (these two forms were in widespread use in small and medium-sized cities by 1920).

REFORM IN STATE GOVERNMENTS

The reform movement spread almost at once to the state level, for it was in state capitals that important decisions affecting the cities were made. Entrenched and very professional political organizations, generously financed by officeholders and businessmen wanting special privileges, controlled most state governments in the late 1890s; everywhere, these organizations were challenged by a rising generation of young and idealistic antiorganization leaders, ambitious for power. They were most successful in the Midwest, under such leaders as Robert M. La Follette of Wisconsin, but they had counterparts all over the country—e.g., Charles Evans Hughes of New York, Woodrow Wilson of New Jersey, Andrew J. Montague of Virginia, and Hiram W. Johnson of California.

Robert M. La Follette. Library of Congress Prints and Photographs Division

Document: Amos P. Wilder: "Governor La Follette and What He Stands For" (1902)

Between 1900 and 1906 Wisconsin, under its governor, Robert M. La Follette, was the leading example of progressivism on the state level. During his first term, La Follette attracted nationwide attention by his efforts to place more political control in the hands of the people. In his campaign for reelection in 1902, he pledged that he would continue to work for direct primary elections to nominate candidates for state offices. (The measure was passed the next year.) Journalist Amos Wilder surveyed the Wisconsin situation in an article for Outlook *magazine in the spring of 1902 and in the process summed up La Follette's political career to that time.*

In Wisconsin the political issues are two: the direct vote in making nominations, thus bringing political control back to the people; and the forcing of corporations to bear their share of taxation. A most trustworthy state Tax Commission reported a year ago that tax reform should begin by adding over $1,200,000 every two years to the amounts already paid by the railroads. The last legislature refused to enact the increase. Can a legislature be secured that will do its duty?

Wisconsin people are not more Populistic than other well-fed, genial Americans who tolerate bathtubs in their homes and accept Carnegie libraries. But many of them believe that the unfolding life of the nation reveals new dangers to guard against; and it has not escaped attention that the nominating of candidates has become a confused and remote process, and that too often the men of power in political councils are the controlling forces in quasi-public corporations which desire favorable legislation. Wealth seeks to fortify itself with all the concomitants of ability, power, and secrecy. Personality is at work, both coercive and persuasive. There is intrigue, indecision, and the play of vice on weakness. The fighters are taking their posts. There is the cry of challenge and defiance.

Meanwhile, the electorate, a body of over 450,000 voters, mostly agriculturists—men of Wisconsin, sons of New England, Germans, Norwegians, and representatives of many other lands—look confusedly on, waiting for the contest to begin. As in all war, the people pay the bills, carry the burdens, and suffer the distress, but they may also profit by a victory. Governor La Follette, whose reelection is the issue, insists that their interests lie his way....

These young leaders revolutionized the art and practice of politics in the United States, not only by exercising strong leadership but also by effecting institutional changes such as the direct primary, direct election of senators (rather than by state legislatures), the initiative, referendum, and recall—which helped restore and revitalize political democracy. More important, perhaps, progressives to a large degree achieved their economic and social objectives—among them, strict regulation of intrastate railroads and public utilities, legislation to prevent child labour and to protect women workers, penal reform, expanded charitable services to the poor, and accident insurance systems to provide compensation to workers and their families.

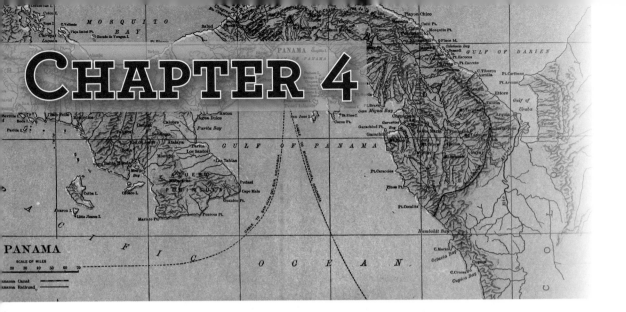

CHAPTER 4

THEODORE ROOSEVELT'S PROGRESSIVISM AND WILLIAM HOWARD TAFT'S TROUBLES

By 1901 the reform upheaval was too strong to be contained within state boundaries. Moreover, certain problems that only the federal government was apparently competent to solve cried out for solution. McKinley might have succeeded in ignoring the rising tide of public opinion had he served out his second term, but McKinley's assassination in September 1901 brought to the presidency an entirely different kind of man—Theodore Roosevelt, at age 42 the youngest man yet to enter the White House.

THE "BULLY PULPIT"

Roosevelt had broad democratic sympathies; moreover, thanks to his experience as police commissioner of New York

Members of a committee governing the Industrial Workers of the World in New York. Library of Congress, Washington, D.C.

City and governor of New York state, he was the first president to have an intimate knowledge of modern urban problems. Because Congress was securely controlled by a group of archconservative Republicans, the new president had to feel his way cautiously in legislative matters; but he emerged full-grown as a tribune of the people after his triumph in the presidential election of 1904. By 1906 he was the undisputed spokesman of national progressivism and by far its best publicity agent. (The White House was, he said, "a bully pulpit.") Meanwhile, by his leadership of public opinion and by acting as a spur on Congress, he had revived the

presidency and made it incomparably the most powerful force in national politics.

In 1901, Americans were perhaps most alarmed about the spread of so-called trusts, or industrial combinations, which they thought were responsible for the steady price increases that had occurred each year since 1897. Ever alert to the winds of public opinion, Roosevelt responded by activating the Sherman Anti-Trust Act of 1890, which had lain dormant because of Cleveland's and McKinley's refusal to enforce it and also because of the Supreme Court's ruling of 1895 that the measure did not apply to combinations in manufacturing. Beginning in 1902 with

Document: Manifesto of the Industrial Workers of the World (1905)

The Industrial Workers of the World, otherwise known as the "Wobblies," was organized in Chicago in 1905. Among the union's founders were William D. ("Big Bill") Haywood of the Western Federation of Miners (WFM), Daniel De Leon of the Socialist Labor Party, and Eugene V. Debs of the Socialist Party. Prior to the founding of the IWW, members of the WFM had called a series of strikes in Cripple Creek, Colo. (1894), Leadville, Colo. (1896), Coeur d'Alene, Idaho (1899), and Telluride, Colo. (1903). The Cripple Creek strike was halted by state militia in 1904, which prompted the WFM to form the first incarnation of the IWW. The difference between this union and the rest of American organized labour was its revolutionary goal of organizing all the world's labour force against the capitalist system, which was to be replaced by a new social order. Founded largely as a protest against the American Federation of Labor, the Wobblies never gained widespread popular support. Their willingness to promote labour strife and violence turned public opinion, as well as the constituted authorities, against them. Their tactics often led to arrests and sensational public-ity; when IWW organizer Joe Hill was executed in 1915 on a disputed murder charge, he became a martyr and folk hero for the labour movement. The organization won its greatest victories in the mining and lumbering industries of the Pacific Northwest. The IWW was the only labour organiza-tion to oppose U.S. participation in World War I, which IWW leaders protested by attempting to limit copper production in western states. The federal government responded by prosecuting and convicting some of those leaders under the newly enacted Sabotage and Espionage Acts. Printed below is the IWW Manifesto, adopted at the first convention. Father Thomas Hagerty, a Roman Catholic priest, is credited with writing part of it; and it was signed by many socialists, including Debs, who eventually rejected the organization.

Social relations and groupings only reflect mechanical and industrial conditions. The great facts of present industry are the displacement of human skill by machines and the increase of capitalist power through concentration in the possession of the tools with which wealth is pro-duced and distributed.

Because of these facts, trade divisions among laborers and competition among capitalists are alike disappearing. Class divisions grow ever more fixed and class antagonisms more sharp. Trade lines have been swallowed up in a common servitude of all workers to the machines which they tend. New machines, ever replacing less productive ones, wipe out whole trades and plunge new bodies of workers into the ever growing army of tradeless, hopeless unemployed. As human beings and human skill are displaced by mechanical progress, the capitalists need use the workers only during that brief period when muscles and nerves respond most intensely. The moment the laborer no longer yields the maximum of profits, he is thrown upon the scrap pile, to starve along-side the discarded machine. A dead line has been drawn, and an age limit established, to cross which, in this world of monopolized opportunities, means condemnation to industrial death....

a suit to dissolve a northwestern railroad monopoly, Roosevelt moved next against the so-called Beef Trust, then against the oil, tobacco, and other monopolies. In every case the Supreme Court supported the administration, going so far in the oil and tobacco decisions of 1911 as to reverse its 1895 decision. In addition, in 1903 Roosevelt persuaded a reluctant Congress to establish a Bureau of Corporations with sweeping power to investigate business practices. The bureau's thoroughgoing reports were of immense assistance in antitrust cases. While establishing the supremacy of the federal government in the industrial field, Roosevelt in 1902 also took action unprecedented in the history of the presidency by intervening on labour's behalf to force the arbitration of a strike by the United Mine Workers of America against the Pennsylvania anthracite coal operators.

Roosevelt moved much more aggressively after his 1904 election. Public demand for effective national regulation of interstate railroad rates had been growing since the Supreme Court had weakened the Interstate Commerce Commission's (ICC) rate-making authority in the 1890s. Determined to bring the railroads—the country's single greatest private economic interest—under effective national control, Roosevelt waged an unrelenting battle with Congress in 1905–06. The outcome—the Hepburn Act of 1906—was his own personal triumph; it greatly enlarged the ICC's jurisdiction and forbade railroads to increase rates without its approval. By using the same

Upton Sinclair's The Jungle, *which is advertised in the poster shown here, was critical in alerting the public to the poor treatment of labour and the unsanitary conditions of the meat-packing industry. Public response spurred the government to enact stricter regulations and health standards.* Library of Congress Prints and Photographs Division

tactics of aggressive leadership, Roosevelt in 1906 also obtained passage of a Meat Inspection Act and a Pure Food and Drug Act. Passage of these acts was aided by the work of Harvey W. Wiley and Sen. Albert J. Beveridge, along with publication of

Muckrakers

The muckrakers were a group of American writers who provided detailed, accurate journalistic accounts of the political and economic corruption and social hardships caused by the power of big business in a rapidly industrializing United States before World War I. The name muckraker was pejorative when used by President Roosevelt in his speech of April 14, 1906; he borrowed a passage from John Bunyan's Pilgrim's Progress, *which referred to "the Man with the Muckrake...who could look no way but downward." But muckraker also came to take on favourable connotations of social concern and courageous exposition.*

The muckrakers' work grew out of the yellow journalism of the 1890s, which whetted the public appetite for news arrestingly presented, and out of popular magazines, especially those established by S.S. McClure, Frank A. Munsey, and Peter F. Collier. The emergence of muckraking was heralded in the January 1903 issue of McClure's Magazine by articles on municipal government, labour, and trusts, written by Lincoln Steffens, Ray Stannard Baker, and Ida M. Tarbell.

The intense public interest aroused by articles critical of political corruption, industrial monopolies, and fraudulent business practices rallied journalists, novelists, and reformers of all sorts to sharpen their criticism of American society. Charles Edward Russell led the reform writers with exposés ranging from The Greatest Trust in the World *(1905) to* The Uprising of the Many *(1907), the latter reporting methods being tried to extend democracy in other countries. Steffens wrote on corrupt city and state politics in* The Shame of the Cities *(1904). Brand Whitlock, who wrote The* Turn of the Balance *(1907), a novel opposing capital punishment, was also a reform mayor of Toledo, Ohio. Thomas W. Lawson, a Boston financier, in "Frenzied Finance" (Everybody's, 1904–05), provided a major exposé of stock-market abuses and insurance fraud. Tarbell's* History of the Standard Oil Company *(1904) exposed the corrupt practices used to form a great industrial monopoly. Edwin Markham's* Children in Bondage *was a major attack on child labour. David Graham Phillips's series "The Treason of the Senate" (Cosmopolitan, 1906), which inspired President Roosevelt's speech in 1906, was influential in leading to the passage of the Seventeenth Amendment to the Constitution, providing for popular senatorial elections. Muckraking as a movement largely disappeared between 1910 and 1912.*

Samuel Hopkins Adams's *Great American Fraud* (1906) and Upton Sinclair's *The Jungle* (1906). Sinclair's famous novel, one of the landmarks of muckraking literature, revealed in gory detail the unsanitary conditions of the Chicago stockyards and meat-packing plants.

Meanwhile, almost from his accession to the presidency, Roosevelt had been carrying on a crusade, often independent of Congress, to conserve the country's fast-dwindling natural resources and to make them available for use under rigorous national supervision. He withdrew from the public domain some 148,000,000 acres of forest lands, 80,000,000 acres of mineral lands, and 1,500,000 acres of water-power sites. Moreover, adoption of the National Reclamation Act of 1902 made possible the beginning of an ambitious federal program of irrigation and hydroelectric development in the West.

TAFT'S PRESIDENCY

Roosevelt was so much the idol of the masses of 1908 that he could have easily gained the Republican nomination in that year. After his election in 1904, however, he had announced that he would not be a candidate four years later; adhering stubbornly to his pledge, he arranged the nomination of his secretary of war, William Howard Taft of Ohio, who easily defeated Bryan, the Democratic candidate.

Taft might have made an ideal president during a time of domestic tranquility, but his tenure in the White House was far from peaceful. National progressivism was nearly at high tide, and a large group of Republican progressives, called "insurgents," sat in both houses of Congress.

"Saved"; cartoon by W. A. Rogers for the New York Herald, *1909. Pres. William Howard Taft protects Speaker of the House Joseph Cannon, whose support he seeks for tariff reform, from insurgent Congressmen.* Library of Congress, Washington, D.C.

The Republican Insurgents

These Republicans, like a majority of Americans, demanded such reforms as tariff reductions, an income tax, the direct election of senators, and even stricter railroad and corporation regulations. Taft, who had strongly supported Roosevelt's policies, thought of himself as a progressive. Actually he was temperamentally and philosophically a conservative; moreover, he lacked the qualities of a dynamic popular leader. In the circumstances, his ineptness,

Document: William Howard Taft: Defense of a High Tariff (1909)

In the special session of Congress that newly elected Pres. William Howard Taft called to address the tariff, the House reported a bill that lowered most duties, but the Senate added over 800 amendments, and the final rates were little lower than in previous years. In spite of strong Midwestern opposition, the Payne-Aldrich Tariff was passed. Taft not only signed the bill, but in a speech at Winona, Minn., on Sept. 17, 1909, a portion of which is reprinted here, he also defended it as "the best tariff bill" ever passed. The result of the speech was to further splinter the Republican Party into conservative and progressive factions.

As long ago as August 1906, in the congressional campaign in Maine, I ventured to announce that I was a tariff revisionist and thought that the time had come for a readjustment of the schedules. I pointed out that it had been ten years prior to that time that the Dingley Bill had been passed; that great changes had taken place in the conditions surrounding the productions of the farm, the factory, and the mine, and that under the theory of protection in that time the rates imposed in the Dingley Bill in many instances might have become excessive; that is, might have been greater than the difference between the cost of production abroad and the cost of production at home, with a sufficient allowance for a reasonable rate of profit to the American producer.

I said that the party was divided on the issue, but that in my judgment the opinion of the party was crystallizing and would probably result in the near future in an effort to make such revision. I pointed out the difficulty that there always was in a revision of the tariff, due to the threatened disturbance of industries to be affected and the suspension of business, in a way which made it unwise to have too many revisions.

In the summer of 1907 my position on the tariff was challenged, and I then entered into a somewhat fuller discussion of the matter. It was contended by the so-called standpatters that rates beyond the necessary measure of protection were not objectionable because behind the tariff wall competition always reduced the prices and thus saved the consumer. But I pointed out in that speech what seems to me as true today as it then was, that the danger of excessive rates was in the temptation they created to form monopolies in the protected articles, and thus to take advantage of the excessive rates by increasing the prices, and therefore, and in order to avoid such a danger, it was wise at regular intervals to examine the question of what the effect of the rates had been upon the industries in this country, and whether the conditions with respect to the cost of production here had so changed as to warrant a reduction in the tariff, and to make a lower rate truly protective of the industry....

indecision, and failure to lead could only spell disaster for his party.

Taft's troubles began when he called Congress into special session in 1909 to take up the first item on his agenda—tariff reform. The measure that emerged from Congress actually increased rates. Republican insurgents and a majority of Americans were outraged, but Taft signed the bill.

Conflicts and misunderstandings over conservation and legislative procedure caused the rift between Taft Republicans and the insurgents to grow. By 1910 the Republican insurgents were clearly in the ascendancy in the Congress. Taking control of the president's railroad-regulation measure, they added new provisions that greatly enlarged the ICC's authority. The following year they bitterly opposed Taft's measure for tariff reciprocity with Canada; it passed with Democratic support in Congress, only to go down to defeat at the hands of the Canadian electorate.

THE 1912 ELECTION

Republican insurgents were determined to prevent Taft's renomination in 1912. They found their leader in Roosevelt, who had become increasingly alienated from Taft and who made a whirlwind campaign for the presidential nomination in the winter and spring of 1912. Roosevelt swept the presidential primaries, even in Taft's own state of Ohio; however, Taft and conservative Republicans controlled the powerful state organizations and the Republican National Committee and were able to nominate Taft by a narrow margin. Convinced that the bosses had stolen the nomination from him, Roosevelt led his followers out of the Republican convention. In August they organized the Progressive ("Bull Moose") Party and named Roosevelt to lead the third-party cause.

Democrats had swept the 1910 congressional and gubernatorial elections; and, after the disruption of the Republican Party in the spring of 1912, it was obvious that almost any passable Democrat could win the presidency in that year. Woodrow Wilson, former president of Princeton University, who had made a brilliant Progressive record as governor of New Jersey, was nominated by the Democrats on the 46th ballot.

Taft's single objective in the 1912 campaign was to defeat Roosevelt. The real contest was between Roosevelt and Wilson for control of the Progressive majority. Campaigning strenuously on a platform that he called the New Nationalism, Roosevelt demanded effective control of big business through a strong federal commission, radical tax reform, and a whole series of measures to put the federal government squarely into the business of social and economic reform.

By contrast Wilson seemed conservative with a program he called the New Freedom; it envisaged a concerted effort to

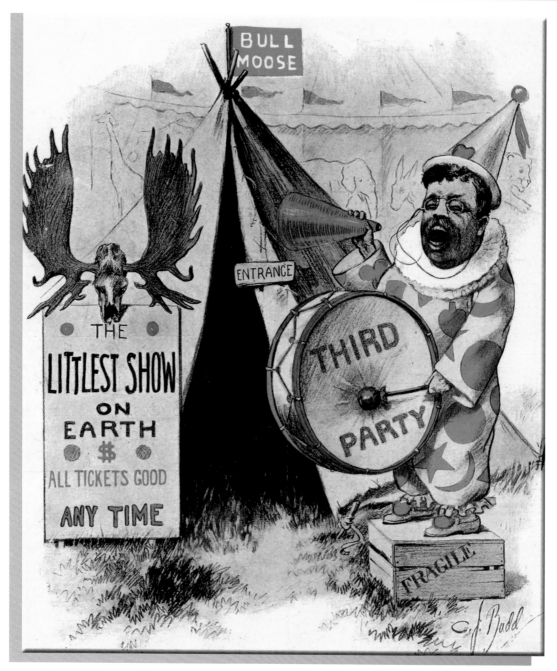

An illustration from the cover of Harper's Weekly. *Although Theodore Roosevelt had already served as president and maintained wide support, he failed to procure the Republican nomination for the 1912 presidential election and ran instead as a candidate of the Progressive Party, also called the Bull Moose Party.* Stock Montage/Archive Photos/Getty Images

Document: Theodore Roosevelt: The New Nationalism (1910)

Many heralded the speech that Roosevelt made on Aug. 31, 1910, at the dedication of the John Brown Battlefield at Osawatomie, Kan., as the beginning of his bid for the 1912 presidential nomination. Adopting Herbert Croly's phrase "new nationalism," Roosevelt outlined a program for widespread reform. Roosevelt's progressive sympathies are revealed in his stand for a "square deal" for the common man, a demand that, when it was made for labour in 1906, had enhanced his popularity. The speech, reprinted here in part, reflected his belief in a strong executive and contained his mature thinking on the responsibility of government to deal with social problems. It is widely considered one of the most influential speeches in American political history.

I stand for the square deal. But when I say that I am for the square deal, I mean not merely that I stand for fair play under the present rules of the game but that I stand for having those rules changed so as to work for a more substantial equality of opportunity and of reward for equally good service. One word of warning, which, I think, is hardly necessary in Kansas. When I say I want a square deal for the poor man, I do not mean that I want a square deal for the man who remains poor because he has not got the energy to work for himself. If a man who has had a chance will not make good, then he has got to quit. And you men of the Grand Army, you want justice for the brave man who fought and punishment for the coward who shirked his work. Is not that so?

Now, this means that our government, national and state, must be freed from the sinister influence or control of special interests....We must drive the special interests out of politics. That is one of our tasks today. Every special interest is entitled to justice—full, fair, and complete—and, now, mind you, if there were any attempt by mob violence to plunder and work harm to the special interest, whatever it may be, that I most dislike, and the wealthy man, whomsoever he may be, for whom I have the greatest contempt, I would fight for him, and you would if you were worth your salt. He should have justice. For every special interest is entitled to justice, but not one is entitled to a vote in Congress, to a voice on the bench, or to representation in any public office. The Constitution guarantees protection to property, and we must make that promise good. But it does not give the right of suffrage to any corporation....

destroy monopoly and to open the doors of economic opportunity to small businessmen through drastic tariff reduction, banking reform, and severe tightening of the antitrust laws. Roosevelt outpolled Taft in the election, but he failed to win many Democratic Progressives away from Wilson, who won by a huge majority of electoral votes, though receiving only about 42 percent of the popular vote.

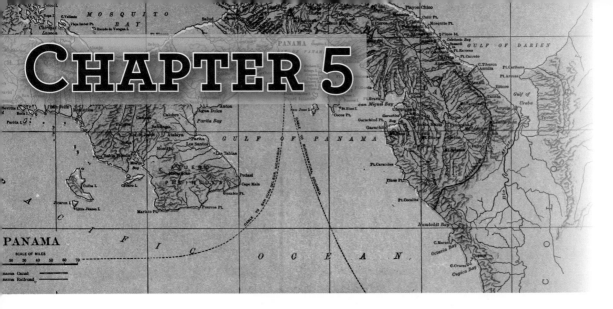

CHAPTER 5

WOODROW WILSON: THE PRESIDENT AS PRIME MINISTER

The presidency offered Wilson his supreme chance to put to work the ideas about government he had advanced first as an academic and then as governor. Wilson's first book, *Congressional Government: A Study in American Politics* (1885), which was based on his doctoral thesis, compared American and parliamentary government and suggested reforms that would make the American system more efficient and more answerable to public opinion. Admitting that he intended to conduct himself as a prime minister, he drew up a legislative program in advance, broke with previous presidential practice by appearing before Congress in person, and worked mainly through his party. Important help in keeping congressional Democrats in line came from the party's three-time unsuccessful presidential nominee, William Jennings Bryan, whom Wilson appointed secretary of state. Indispensable policy advice came from the controversial Boston attorney Louis D. Brandeis, who had helped Wilson formulate the New Freedom agenda during the campaign. Wilson also kept Congress in session continually from April 1913 to October 1914, almost a year and a half, something that had never before happened, not even during the Civil War.

Woodrow Wilson. Library of Congress Prints and Photographs Division

THE NEW FREEDOM AND ITS TRANSFORMATION

Trained as a political scientist and historian, Wilson believed that the president should be the leader of public opinion, the chief formulator of legislative policy, and virtually sovereign in the conduct of foreign relations. With the support of an aroused public opinion and a compliant Democratic majority, he was able to put his theories of leadership into effect with spectacular success.

The first item in Wilson's program was tariff reform, a perennial Democratic objective since the Civil War; the president's measure, the Underwood Tariff Act of 1913, reduced average rates from 40 percent to 25 percent, greatly

Document: Woodrow Wilson: First Inaugural Address (1913)

Wilson was sworn in as the 28th president of the United States on March 4, 1913. His first inaugural address, sometimes compared to Thomas Jefferson's first and to Abraham Lincoln's second, outlined the broad changes that he proposed for the country during the next four years. Interpreting his victory (despite his popular minority) as a mandate to clean house in Washington and especially to rid the government of the influence of privileged groups, Wilson pledged himself to reform the banking system and to lower tariffs. In November 1914 Wilson pointed to the passage during the previous 13 months of the Underwood Tariff Act, the Federal Reserve Act, the Clayton Antitrust Act, and the Federal Trade Commission Act as evidence that the main goals of progressivism had been accomplished. But writer Herbert Croly complained in The New Republic *that the president had "utterly misconceived the meaning and the task of American progressivism" and had surrounded his misconception "with a halo of shimmering rhetoric." This disagreement highlights the multifaceted nature of progressivism, which clearly meant different things to different people.*

There has been a change of government. It began two years ago, when the House of Representatives became Democratic by a decisive majority. It has now been completed. The Senate about to assemble will also be Democratic. The offices of President and Vice-President have been put into the hands of Democrats. What does the change mean? That is the question that is uppermost in our minds today. That is the question I am going to try to answer in order, if I may, to interpret the occasion.

It means much more than the mere success of a party. The success of a party means little except when the nation is using that party for a large and definite purpose. No one can mistake the purpose for which the nation now seeks to use the Democratic Party. It seeks to use it to interpret a change in its own plans and point of view. Some old things with which we had grown familiar, and which had begun to creep into the very habit of our thought and of our lives, have altered their aspect as we have latterly looked critically upon them with fresh, awakened eyes; have dropped their disguises and shown themselves alien and sinister. Some new things, as we look frankly upon them, willing to comprehend their real character, have come to assume the aspect of things long believed in and familiar, stuff of our own convictions. We have been refreshed by a new insight into our own life....

enlarged the free list, and included a modest income tax. Next came adoption of the president's measure for banking and monetary reform, the Federal Reserve Act of 1913, which created a federal reserve system to mobilize banking reserves and issue a flexible new currency—federal reserve notes—based on gold and commercial paper; uniting and supervising the entire system was a federal reserve board of presidential appointees.

The third, and Wilson thought the last, part of the New Freedom program was antitrust reform. In his first significant movement toward Roosevelt's New Nationalism, Wilson reversed his position that merely strengthening the Sherman

Anti-Trust Act would suffice to prevent monopoly. Instead, he took up and pushed through Congress the Progressive-sponsored Federal Trade Commission Act of 1914. It established an agency—the Federal Trade Commission (FTC)—with sweeping authority to prevent business practices that would lead to monopoly.

Meanwhile, Wilson had abandoned his original measure, the Clayton Anti-Trust Act passed by Congress in 1914—its severe provisions against interlocking directorates and practices tending toward monopoly had been gravely weakened by the time the president signed it. The Clayton Act included a declaration that labour unions, as such, were not to be construed as conspiracies in restraint of trade in violation of the antitrust laws, but what organized labour wanted, and did not get, was immunity from prosecution for such measures as the sympathetic strike and the secondary boycott, which the courts had proscribed as violations of the Sherman Act.

In a public letter in November 1914, the president announced that his reform program was complete. But

Document: Louis D. Brandeis: The Money Trust (1913)

Using the statistical evidence presented by the Pujo Committee Report on business consolidation, Louis D. Brandeis, the noted progressive attorney and friend of Woodrow Wilson, wrote a series of articles for Harper's Weekly *in 1913. In his first article, on the "money trust," Brandeis described the operations of the investment banker, showing how firms such as J. P. Morgan & Co. were able to control a vast network of companies by pyramiding their financial holdings.*

The dominant element in our financial oligarchy is the investment banker. Associated banks, trust companies, and life insurance companies are his tools. Controlled railroads, public-service and industrial corporations are his subjects. Though properly but middlemen, these bankers bestride as masters America's business world, so that practically no large enterprise can be undertaken successfully without their participation or approval. These bankers are, of course, able men possessed of large fortunes; but the most potent factor in their control of business is not the possession of extraordinary ability or huge wealth. The key to their power is combination—concentration, intensive and comprehensive—advancing on three distinct lines:

First, there is the obvious consolidation of banks and trust companies; the less obvious affiliations—through stockholdings, voting trusts, and interlocking directorates—of banking institutions which are not legally connected; and the joint transactions, gentlemen's agreements, and "banking ethics" which eliminate competition among the investment bankers.

Second, there is the consolidation of railroads into huge systems, the large combinations of public-service corporations and the formation of industrial trusts, which, by making business so "big" that local, independent banking concerns cannot alone supply the necessary funds, has created dependence upon the associated New York bankers.

But combination, however intensive, along these lines only, could not have produced the money trust—another and more potent factor of combination was added....

Louis Brandeis. Library of Congress Prints and Photographs Division

various groups were still demanding the advanced kind of social and economic legislation that Roosevelt had advocated in 1912. Also, by early 1916 the Progressive Party had largely disintegrated, and Wilson knew that he could win reelection only with the support of a substantial minority of Roosevelt's former followers. Consequently—and also because his own political thinking had been moving toward a more advanced Progressive position—Wilson struck out upon a new political course in 1916. He began by appointing Louis D. Brandeis, the leading critic of big business and finance, to the Supreme Court.

Then in quick succession he obtained passage of a rural-credits measure to supply cheap long-term credit to farmers; anti-child-labour and federal workmen's-compensation legislation; the Adamson Act, establishing the eight-hour day for interstate railroad workers; and measures for federal aid to education and highway construction. With such a program behind him, Wilson was able to rally a new coalition of Democrats, former Progressives, independents, social workers, and a large minority of Socialists; and he narrowly defeated his Republican opponent, Charles Evans Hughes, in the 1916 presidential election.

WOODROW WILSON AND INTERVENTION IN THE MEXICAN REVOLUTION

Although Wilson's consuming interest was in domestic politics, he had to deal primarily with foreign affairs while in the White House; and before the end of his presidency he had developed into a diplomatist of great skill as well as one of the commanding figures in world affairs. He was a "strong" president in the conduct of foreign policy, writing most of the important diplomatic correspondence of his government and making all important decisions himself. He usually worked well with his secretaries of state, Bryan and Robert Lansing, and often relied for advice upon his confidential counselor, Col. Edward M. House of Texas.

Wilson served his apprenticeship by having to deal at the outset of his administration with an uprising in Mexico, set off when a military usurper, Victoriano Huerta, murdered liberal president Francisco Madero and seized the executive power in February 1913. It was difficult for the United States to remain aloof because Americans had invested heavily in Mexico and 40,000 U.S. citizens resided there.

If Wilson had followed conventional policy and the urgings of Americans with interests in Mexico, he would have recognized Huerta (as most European governments did), who promised to respect and protect all foreign investments and concessions. But Wilson was revolted by Huerta's bloody rise to power; moreover, he believed that the revolution begun by Madero in 1910 was a glorious episode in the history of human liberty.

Wilson thus not only refused to recognize Huerta but also tried to persuade the dictator to step down from office and permit the holding of free elections for a new democratic government. When Huerta refused to cooperate, Wilson gave open support to the Constitutionalists—Huerta's opponents under Madero's successor, Venustiano Carranza—and, when it seemed that the Constitutionalists could not themselves drive Huerta from power, Wilson seized the port of Veracruz in April 1914 to cut off Huerta's supplies and revenues. This stratagem succeeded, and Carranza and his army occupied Mexico City in August.

The revolutionary forces then divided between Carranza's followers and those of his chief rival and most colorful general, Pancho Villa, and civil war raged for another year. Wilson refused to interfere. Carranza emerged victorious by the summer of 1915, and Wilson accorded him de facto recognition in October. In January 1916, however, Villa

Document: Woodrow Wilson: The Tampico Affair (1914)

Mexico, in 1913, had been the scene of a military coup led by Gen. Victoriano Huerta, whose regime U.S. President Woodrow Wilson refused to recognize because it was, in his words, a "government of butchers." A crisis developed in April 1914 when some crew members of the U.S.S. Dolphin *were arrested in Tampico, where the American ship had docked. Although the sailors were released immediately and an apology was extended, Adm. Henry T. Mayo, commander of the American fleet off Veracruz, demanded a 21-gun salute to the American flag. When the salute was refused, the president went before Congress on April 20 to ask for permission to demand satisfaction from the Huerta administration. Wilson finally accepted an offer by Argentina, Brazil, and Chile (thereafter known as the ABC powers) to mediate, and war was averted. Wilson's message of April 20 appears below.*

It is my duty to call your attention to a situation which has arisen in our dealings with General Victoriano Huerta at Mexico City which calls for action, and to ask your advice and cooperation in acting upon it.

On the 9th of April a paymaster of the U.S.S. *Dolphin* landed at the Iturbide Bridge landing at Tampico with a whaleboat and boat's crew to take off certain supplies needed by his ship, and while engaged in loading the boat was arrested by an officer and squad of men of the army of General Huerta. Neither the paymaster nor anyone of the boat's crew was armed. Two of the men were in the boat when the arrest took place and were obliged to leave it and submit to be taken into custody, notwithstanding the fact that the boat carried, both at her bow and at her stern, the flag of the United States.

The officer who made the arrest was proceeding up one of the streets of the town with his prisoners when met by an officer of higher authority, who ordered him to return to the landing and await orders; and within an hour and a half from the time of the arrest, orders were received from the commander of the Huertista forces at Tampico for the release of the paymaster and his men. The release was followed by apologies from the commander and later by an expression of regret by General Huerta himself....

Pancho Villa riding his horse during the Mexican Revolution. Library of Congress Prints and Photographs Division

executed about 17 U.S. citizens at Santa Isabel to demonstrate Carranza's lack of control in northern Mexico. Then, seeking to provoke war between the United States and Mexico, he raided Columbus, N. M., on March 9, 1916, burning the town and killing some 17 inhabitants. Wilson sent a punitive expedition under Gen. John J. Pershing into Mexico in hot pursuit of Villa; but the wily guerrilla eluded Pershing, and, the deeper the U.S. forces penetrated into Mexican territory, the more agitated the Carranza government became. There were two serious skirmishes between regular Mexican and U.S. troops in the spring, and full-scale war was averted only when Wilson withdrew Pershing's column some months later. Relations between the two governments were greatly improved when Wilson extended de jure recognition to Carranza's new Constitutional regime in April 1917. Thereafter, Wilson adamantly rejected all further foreign and American suggestions for intervention in Mexico.

CHAPTER 6

"OVER THERE": THE UNITED STATES AND WORLD WAR I

World War I was one of the great watersheds of 20th-century geopolitical history. The war pitted the Central Powers—mainly Germany, Austria-Hungary, and Turkey—against the Allies—mainly France, Great Britain, Russia, Italy, Japan, and, from 1917, the United States. It ended with the defeat of the Central Powers. The war was virtually unprecedented in the slaughter, carnage, and destruction it caused. It led to the fall of four great imperial dynasties (in Germany, Russia, Austria-Hungary, and Turkey), resulted in the Bolshevik Revolution in Russia, and, in its destabilization of European society, laid the groundwork for World War II. The entry of the United States was the turning point of the war because it made the eventual defeat of Germany possible. It had been foreseen in 1916 that if the United States went to war, the Allies' military effort against Germany would be upheld by U.S. supplies and by enormous extensions of credit. These expectations were amply and decisively fulfilled. But it took Americans more than a while to decide that they were ready to enter the fray.

Document: George M. Cohan: "Over There" (1917)

"Over There" was actor and songwriter George M. Cohan's main contribution to the U.S. war effort—and no mean contribution it was. Enrico Caruso sang it on the steps of the New York Public Library and sold thousands of dollars worth of Liberty Bonds, and it was adopted by the men of the American Expeditionary Force as their favorite marching song. Congress authorized Cohan a special medal for the song in 1940, and it was sung by a new generation of American soldiers in World War II.

Legion Airs: Songs of the Armed Forces, *Lee O. Smith, ed., New York, 1960.*

OVER THERE

Johnnie get your gun, get your gun, get your gun,
Take it on the run, on the run, on the run;
Hear them calling you and me;
Every son of liberty.
Hurry right away, no delay, go today,
Make your daddy glad, to have had such a lad,
Tell your sweetheart not to pine,
To be proud her boy's in line.

Chorus:

Over there, over there,
Send the word, send the word over there,
That the Yanks are coming, the Yanks are coming,
The drums rum-tumming everywhere.
So prepare, say a prayer,
Send the word, send the word to beware,
We'll be over, we're coming over,
And we won't come back till it's over over there.

Johnnie get your gun, get your gun, get your gun,
Johnnie show the Hun, you're a son-of-a-gun,
Hoist the flag and let her fly,
Like true heroes do or die.
Pack your little kit, show your grit, do your bit,
Soldiers to the ranks from the towns and the tanks,
Make your mother proud of you,
And to liberty be true.

THE STRUGGLE FOR NEUTRALITY

The outbreak of general war in Europe in August 1914 raised grave challenges to Wilson's skill and leadership in foreign affairs. In spite of the appeals of propagandists for the rival Allies and Central Powers, the great majority of Americans were doggedly neutral and determined to avoid involvement unless American rights and interests were grossly violated. This, too, was Wilson's own feeling, and in August he issued an official proclamation of neutrality and two weeks later appealed to Americans to be "impartial in thought as well as in action."

LOANS AND SUPPLIES FOR THE ALLIES

Difficulties arose first with the British government, which at once used its vast fleet to establish a long-range blockade of Germany. The U.S. State Department sent several strong protests to London, particularly against British suppression of American exports of food and raw materials to Germany. Anglo-American blockade controversies were not acute, however, because the British put their blockade controls into effect gradually, always paid for goods seized, argued persuasively that in a total war food and raw materials were as essential as guns and ammunition, and pointed out that they, the British, were simply following

blockade precedents established by the United States itself during the American Civil War. As a result of a tacit Anglo-American agreement, the United States soon became the chief external source of supply for the food, raw materials, and munitions that fed the British and French war machines. In addition, and in accordance with the strict rules of neutrality, the Wilson administration permitted the Allied governments to borrow more than $2,000,000,000 in the United States in order to finance the war trade. At the same time, the president resisted all efforts by German Americans for an arms embargo on the ground that such a measure would be grossly unneutral toward the Allies.

GERMAN SUBMARINE WARFARE

There was no possibility of conflict between Germany and the United States so long as the former confined its warfare to the continent of Europe; a new situation full of potential danger arose, however, when the German authorities decided to use their new weapon, the submarine, to challenge British control of the seas. The German admiralty announced in February 1915 that all Allied vessels would be torpedoed without warning in a broad area and that even neutral vessels were not safe. Wilson replied at once that he would hold Germany to "strict accountability" (a conventional diplomatic term) if submarines destroyed American ships and lives without warning. The Germans soon gave broad

A German submarine, or U-boat (undersea boat), sitting at a dock. Hulton Archive/Getty Images

guarantees concerning American ships, and their safety against illegal submarine attacks was not an issue between the two countries before 1917.

An issue much more fraught with danger was the safety of Americans traveling and working on Allied ships. A German submarine sank the unarmed British liner *Lusitania* without warning on May 7, 1915, killing 1,198 passengers and crew, including 128 Americans. Wilson at first appealed to the Germans on broad grounds of humanity to abandon submarine warfare, but in the subsequent negotiations he narrowed the issue to one of safety for unarmed passenger liners against violent underseas attack.

Momentary resolution came when a submarine sank the unarmed British liner *Arabic* in August. Wilson warned

The front page of the New York Times *after the* Lusitania *had been sunk by a German submarine.*
MPI/Archive Photos/Getty Images

Document: William Jennings Bryan: American Protest Over the Sinking of the *Lusitania* (1915)

The American people were indignant at the sinking of the Lusitania *and demanded strong action against Germany. Although President Wilson observed that "there is such a thing as a man being too proud to fight," he agreed with his advisers, including Secretary of State Bryan, that a protest note must be sent. Bryan, an avowed pacifist, was reluctant to issue too strong a rebuke for fear that it would draw the United States into the war. But he sent the following note on May 13, 1915, to the U.S. ambassador in Germany. This was the first of three so-called* Lusitania *Notes.*

Please call on the minister of foreign affairs and, after reading to him this communication, leave him with a copy.

In view of recent acts of the German authorities in violation of American rights on the high seas which culminated in the torpedoing and sinking of the British steamship *Lusitania* on May 7, 1915, by which over 100 American citizens lost their lives, it is clearly wise and desirable that the government of the United States and the Imperial German government should come to a clear and full understanding as to the grave situation which has resulted.

The sinking of the British passenger steamer *Falaba* by a German submarine on March 28, through which Leon C. Thrasher, an American citizen, was drowned; the attack on April 28 on the American vessel *Cushing* by a German aeroplane; the torpedoing on May 1 of the American vessel *Gulflight* by a German submarine, as a result of which two or more American citizens met their death; and, finally, the torpedoing and sinking of the steamship *Lusitania* constitute a series of events which the government of the United States has observed with growing concern, distress, and amazement....

that he would break diplomatic relations if such attacks continued, and the Germans grudgingly promised not to attack unarmed passenger ships without warning. The controversy escalated to a more dangerous level when a submarine torpedoed the packet steamer *Sussex* in the English Channel with heavy loss of life in March 1916. In an ultimatum to Berlin, Wilson threatened to break diplomatic relations if the Germans did not cease attacking liners and merchantmen without warning; once again the Germans capitulated, but they threatened to resume unrestricted submarine warfare if the United States failed to force the British to observe international law in their blockade practices.

The Allies complicated the submarine controversy in late 1915 by arming many of their liners and merchantmen sailing to American ports. Wilson tried to arrange a compromise by which the Allies would disarm their ships in return for a German promise not to sink them without warning. When the British rejected the proposal, the president gave the impression that he would hold Germany accountable for American lives lost on armed ships, setting off a rebellion in Congress and the near passage of resolutions forbidding American citizens to travel on armed ships. Actually, the president had no intention of permitting armed ships to become a serious issue; their status was never a subject of serious controversy between the United States and Germany.

Arming for War

Meanwhile, the increasingly perilous state of relations with Germany had prompted Wilson, in December 1915, to call for a considerable expansion in the country's armed forces. A violent controversy over preparedness ensued, both in Congress and in the country at large.

The army legislation of 1916 was a compromise, with Wilson obtaining only a modest increase in the army and a strengthening of the National Guard; but the Naval Appropriations Act of 1916

Document: Leonard Wood: Military Unpreparedness (1915)

The German submarine attacks on American and British ships in 1915 convinced many Americans that the only security for the United States lay in a formidable buildup of military power. The "preparedness" advocates, as they were called, argued that the ability to wage war was the first prerequisite of remaining neutral. The argument, of course, cut both ways, and the position was severely criticized by those who maintained that preparedness was in fact the first step toward active involvement in the conflict. Maj. Gen. Leonard Wood, a staunch preparedness advocate, helped organize the "Plattsburgh" volunteers in the summer of 1915. Earlier that year he wrote the book The Military Obligation of Citizenship, *from which the following selection is taken.*

The people of the United States are singularly lacking in information concerning both the military history of their country and its military policy. Students in school and college as a rule receive entirely erroneous ideas on both of these subjects. The average young man, unless he has really made a study of the country's history, is firmly convinced that the Revolutionary War was characterized throughout by the highest quality of patriotism and devotion to the best interests of the country on the part of the people as a whole.

He is not at all familiar with the desperate struggle which was made by Washington, various colonial assemblies, and the Confederation of Colonies to keep in the field even a small force of troops. He hears very little of the bickerings, mutinies, desertions, and frequent changes of personnel which made the war a difficult one to conduct and served to bring out into strong relief the remarkable qualities of Washington—those qualities of patience, good judgment, discretion, and again patience, and more patience, which made it possible for him to hold the illy-equipped, disjointed, and discordant elements together, and to have always available some kind of a fighting force, although seldom an effective one.

We have as a nation neglected the lessons of past wars and have learned little from the example of the great military nations, and, as Emory Upton truthfully says: "Our general policy has followed closely that of China." Perhaps this statement may be somewhat extreme in all which applies to conditions up to the end of the Civil War, but it is not in any way extreme when applied to conditions which exist today. The great nations with policies to uphold and interests to defend have made what they believe to be adequate military preparation....

provided for more ships than the administration had requested.

THE UNITED STATES ENTERS THE GREAT WAR

Wilson's most passionate desire, aside from avoiding belligerency, was to bring an end to the war through his personal mediation. He sent Colonel House to Europe in early 1915 to explore the possibilities of peace and again early in 1916 to press for a plan of Anglo-American cooperation for peace. The British refused to cooperate, and the president, more than ever eager to avoid a final confrontation with Germany on the submarine issue, decided to press forward with independent mediation. He was by this time also angered by the intensification of British blockade practices and convinced that both sides were fighting for world domination and spoils. On Dec. 18, 1916, Wilson asked the belligerents to state the terms upon which they would be willing to make peace. Soon afterward, in secret, high-level negotiations, he appealed to Britain and Germany to hold an early peace conference under his leadership.

BREAK WITH GERMANY

Chances for peace were blasted by a decision of the German leaders, made at an imperial conference on Jan. 9, 1917, to inaugurate an all-out submarine war against all commerce, neutral as well as belligerent. The Germans knew that such a campaign would bring the United States into the war; but they were confident that their augmented submarine fleet could starve Britain into submission before the United States could mobilize and participate effectively.

The announcement of the new submarine blockade in January left the president no alternative but to break diplomatic relations with Germany, which he did on February 3. At the same time, and in subsequent addresses, the president made it clear that he would accept unrestricted submarine warfare against belligerent merchantmen and would act only if American ships were sunk. In early March he put arms on American ships in the hope that this would deter submarine attacks. The Germans began to sink American ships indiscriminately in mid-March, and on April 2 Wilson asked Congress to recognize that a state of war existed between the United States and the German Empire. Congress approved the war resolution quickly, and Wilson signed it on April 6.

MOBILIZATION

Generally speaking, the efforts at mobilization went through two stages. During the first, lasting roughly from April to December 1917, the administration relied mainly on voluntary and cooperative efforts. During the second stage, after December 1917, the government moved rapidly to establish complete control over every important phase of economic

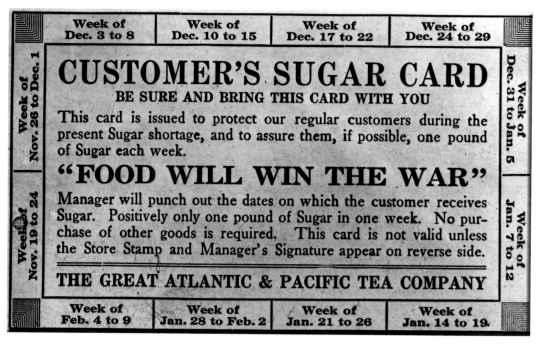

| Week of Dec. 3 to 8 | Week of Dec. 10 to 15 | Week of Dec. 17 to 22 | Week of Dec. 24 to 29 |

CUSTOMER'S SUGAR CARD

BE SURE AND BRING THIS CARD WITH YOU

This card is issued to protect our regular customers during the present Sugar shortage, and to assure them, if possible, one pound of Sugar each week.

"FOOD WILL WIN THE WAR"

Manager will punch out the dates on which the customer receives Sugar. Positively only one pound of Sugar in one week. No purchase of other goods is required. This card is not valid unless the Store Stamp and Manager's Signature appear on reverse side.

THE GREAT ATLANTIC & PACIFIC TEA COMPANY

(Left side, vertical: Week of Nov. 26 to Dec. 1; Week of Nov. 19 to 24)
(Right side, vertical: Week of Dec. 31 to Jan. 5; Week of Jan. 7 to 12)

| Week of Feb. 4 to 9 | Week of Jan. 28 to Feb. 2 | Week of Jan. 21 to 26 | Week of Jan. 14 to 19 |

Sugar ration card used during World War I, 1917. Encyclopædia Britannica, Inc.

life. Railroads were nationalized; a war industries board established ironclad controls over industry; food and fuel were strictly rationed; an emergency-fleet corporation began construction of a vast merchant fleet; and a war labour board used coercive measures to prevent strikes. Opposition to the war was sternly suppressed under the Espionage Act of 1917. At the same time, the Committee on Public Information, headed by the progressive journalist George Creel,

The U.S. government's many propaganda efforts included issuing posters, such as this one, that served to convince Americans of the need for war and to encourage them to contribute to the war effort. MPI/Archive Photos/Getty Images

THE WORLD CANNOT LIVE HALF SLAVE, HALF FREE

THE PRUSSIAN BLOT

EUROPE

100,000,000 PEOPLE ALREADY ENSLAVED BY GERMANY

President Wilson Says of the Germans:
"Their plan was to throw a broad belt of German military power and political control across the very center of Europe and beyond the Mediterranean Sea into the heart of Asia. They have actually carried the greater part of that amazing plan into execution."

THE KAISER PROCLAIMS:
"Woe and death unto those who oppose my will. Death to the infidel who denies my mission. Let all the enemies of the German nation perish. God demands their destruction."

WHILE GERMANY DREAMS OF DOMINATING THE WORLD BY FORCE THERE CAN BE NO PEACE

Document: Charles A. Beard: Reasons for His Resignation from Columbia University (1917)

The patriotic hysteria that swept the country after war was declared in 1917 demanded unques-tioned support of government policies from all segments of the community, on pain of ostracism and, in some cases, even loss of a job. Perhaps because of the long tradition of academic freedom in America, many university faculties reacted to such demands with singular bitterness. When Henry W. L. Dana, an avowed pacifist who worked for the peace movement, was asked to leave Columbia University because of his political beliefs, Professor Charles A. Beard, a historian whose Economic Interpretation of the Constitution *(1913) had brought him national recognition, resigned in protest. His statement was published in* The New Republic *and is reprinted here.*

It has been insinuated by certain authorities of Columbia University that I resigned in a fit of unjustified petulance, and I therefore beg to submit the following statement:

1. My first real experience with the inner administration of the university came with the retirement of Prof. John W. Burgess. For some time before his withdrawal, his work in American constitu-tional law had been carried by Professor X and it was the desire of the members of the faculty that the latter should be appointed Ruggles Professor to succeed Mr. Burgess. But Mr. X had published a book in which he justified criticism of the Supreme Court as a means of bringing our constitu-tional law into harmony with our changing social and economic life. He was therefore excluded from the Ruggles professorship. It was given to Mr. W. D. Guthrie, a successful corporation lawyer, and a partner of one of the trustees of the university.

It was understood that Mr. Guthrie should give one lecture a week for one semester each year in return for the high honor. Mr. Butler is constantly saying that all matters relating to appoint-ment, fitness, and tenure are left to the appropriate faculties, or words to this effect. As a matter of plain fact, the Faculty of Political Science as such was not consulted in advance in the selection of the Ruggles Professor. The whole affair was settled by backstairs negotiation, and it was under-stood by all of us who had any part in the business that no person with progressive or liberal views would be acceptable.

Mr. Guthrie was duly appointed. Of his contributions to learning I shall not speak, but I can say that he did not attend faculty meetings, help in conducting doctors' examinations, or assume the burdens imposed upon other professors. This was the way in which the first important vacancy in the Faculty of Political Science was filled after my connection with the institution....

mobilized publicists, scholars, and oth-ers in a vast prowar propaganda effort. Support for the war among intellectuals and academics was certainly not uni-versal, however. In general, Americans lined up behind the war effort, and by the spring of 1918, the American people and their economy had been harnessed for total war (a near miracle, considering the lack of preparedness only a year before).

An American soldier with a machine gun. Three Lions/Hulton Archive/Getty Images

America's Role in the War

The American military contribution, while small compared to that of the Allies during the entire war, was in two respects decisive in the outcome. The U.S. Navy, fully prepared at the outset, provided the ships that helped the British overcome the submarine threat by the autumn of 1917. The U.S. Army, some 4,000,000 men strong, was raised mainly by conscription under the Selective Service Act of 1917. The American Expeditionary Force of more than 1,200,000 men under General Pershing reached France by September 1918, and this huge infusion of manpower tipped the balance on the Western Front and helped to end the war in November 1918, a year earlier than military planners had anticipated.

Woman Suffrage

World War I, and the major role played in it by women in various capacities, broke down most of the remaining opposition

Suffragettes marching through Manhattan in 1915. Paul Thompson/Hulton Archive/ Getty Images

to woman suffrage in the United States. Amendments to the federal Constitution concerning woman suffrage had been introduced into Congress in 1878 and 1914, but the 1878 amendment had been overwhelmingly defeated, and the 1914 amendment had narrowly failed to gain even a simple majority of the votes in the House of Representatives and the Senate (a two-thirds majority vote in Congress was needed for the amendment to be sent to the state legislatures for ratification). By 1918, however, both major political parties were committed

Document: Susan B. Anthony: "The Status of Woman, Past, Present, and Future" (1897)

By 1897 suffragette Susan B. Anthony had laboured for more than 40 years, along with her friend Elizabeth Cady Stanton, for the right of women to vote. Anthony was a legend in her own time and was admired for her devotion to and perseverance in the cause of woman suffrage. Girls who were tomboys, one author has noted, were called "Susan B's." As cofounder of the National Woman Suffrage Association, she worked for the passage of a federal amendment granting women the vote. The Nineteenth Amendment, often called the Anthony Amendment, was not ratified until 1920, but Anthony displayed, in this article published in 1897 and reprinted here in part, the confidence and optimism that supported her through the many years of struggle.

Fifty years ago woman in the United States was without a recognized individuality in any department of life. No provision was made in public or private schools for her education in anything beyond the rudimentary branches. An educated woman was a rarity and was gazed upon with something akin to awe. The women who were known in the world of letters, in the entire country, could be easily counted upon the ten fingers. Margaret Fuller, educated by her father, a Harvard graduate and distinguished lawyer, stood preeminently at the head and challenged the admiration of such men as Emerson, Channing, and Greeley....

Such was the helpless, dependent, fettered condition of woman when the first Woman's Rights Convention was called just forty-nine years ago, at Seneca Falls, N.Y., by Elizabeth Cady Stanton and Lucretia Mott....

While there had been individual demands, from time to time, the first organized body to formulate a declaration of the rights of women was the one which met at Seneca Falls, July 19–20, 1848, and adjourned to meet at Rochester two weeks later. In the Declaration of Sentiments and the Resolutions there framed, every point was covered that, down to the present day, has been contended for by the advocates of equal rights for women. Every inequality of the existing laws and customs was carefully considered and a thorough and complete readjustment demanded....

to woman suffrage, and the amendment was carried by the necessary two-thirds majorities in both the House and Senate in January 1918 and June 1919, respectively.

Vigorous campaigns were then waged to secure ratification of the amendment by two-thirds of the state legislatures, and on Aug. 18, 1920, Tennessee became the 36th state to ratify the amendment. On August 26 the Nineteenth Amendment was proclaimed by the secretary of state as being part of the Constitution of the United States.

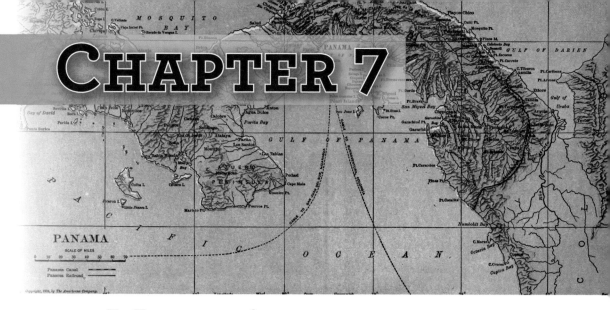

CHAPTER 7

WILSON'S VISION OF A NEW WORLD ORDER

In one of the most ambitious rhetorical efforts in modern history, President Wilson attempted to rally the people of the world in a movement for a peace settlement that would remove the causes of future wars and establish machinery to maintain peace. In an address to the Senate in January 1917, he called for a "peace without victory" to be enforced by a league of nations that the United States would join and strongly support. He reiterated this program in his war message, adding that the United States wanted above all else to "make the world safe for democracy." And when he failed to persuade the British and French leaders to join him in issuing a common statement of war aims, he went to Congress in January 1918, to make, in his Fourteen Points address, his definitive avowal to the American people and the world.

In his general points Wilson demanded an end to the old diplomacy that had led to wars in the past. He proposed open diplomacy instead of entangling alliances, and he called for freedom of the seas, an impartial settlement of colonial claims, general disarmament, removal of artificial trade barriers, and, most important, a league of nations to promote peace and protect the territorial integrity and independence

Document: Woodrow Wilson: Peace Without Victory (1917)

Following his reelection in the fall of 1916 President Wilson renewed his efforts to bring about a negotiated settlement of the war in Europe. On Jan. 22, 1917, less than two weeks after the British had refused a German peace offer on the grounds that it was too vague, the president went before the Senate to try to clarify the American position in the proposed negotiations. Many people rejoiced at his statement, printed here, that the war's end must bring a "peace without victory." Social worker Lillian Wald wrote the president that this speech alone would make him famous and predicted that "liberals of every faith…will be proud as long as men write and speak of these times in which we live."

On the 18th of December last, I addressed an identic note to the governments of the nations now at war requesting them to state, more definitely than they had yet been stated by either group of belligerents, the terms upon which they would deem it possible to make peace. I spoke on behalf of humanity and of the rights of all neutral nations like our own, many of whose most vital interests the war puts in constant jeopardy.

The Central Powers united in a reply which stated merely that they were ready to meet their antagonists in conference to discuss terms of peace. The Entente Powers have replied much more definitely and have stated, in general terms, indeed, but with sufficient definiteness to imply details, the arrangements, guarantees, and acts of reparation which they deem to be the indispensable conditions of a satisfactory settlement. We are that much nearer a definite discussion of the peace which shall end the present war. We are that much nearer the discussion of the international concert which must thereafter hold the world at peace.

In every discussion of the peace that must end this war, it is taken for granted that that peace must be followed by some definite concert of power which will make it virtually impossible that any such catastrophe should ever overwhelm us again. Every lover of mankind, every sane and thoughtful man must take that for granted….

of its members. On specific issues he demanded, among other things, the restoration of a Belgium ravaged by the Germans; sympathetic treatment of the Russians, then involved in a civil war; establishment of an independent Poland; the return of Alsace-Lorraine to France; and autonomy or self-determination for the subject peoples of the Austro-Hungarian and Ottoman empires. A breathtaking pronouncement, the Fourteen Points gave new hope to millions of liberals and moderate socialists who were fighting for a new international order based upon peace and justice.

THE PARIS PEACE CONFERENCE AND THE TREATY OF VERSA

With their armies reeling under the weight of a combined Allied and American assault, the Germans appealed to Wilson in October 1918 for an armistice based on the Fourteen Points and other presidential pronouncements. The Allies agreed to

Document: Woodrow Wilson: Fourteen Points (1918)

In his address to the joint session of the United States Congress on Jan. 8, 1918, President Wilson formulated under 14 separate heads his ideas of the essential nature of a post–World War I settlement. An excerpt from that address, including Wilson's enumeration of the 14 points, is presented here:

We entered this war because violations of right had occurred which touched us to the quick and made the life of our own people impossible unless they were corrected and the world secure once for all against their recurrence What we demand in this war, therefore, is nothing peculiar to ourselves. It is that the world be made fit and safe to live in; and particularly that it be made safe for every peaceloving nation which, like our own, wishes to live its own life, determine its own institutions, be assured of justice and fair dealing by the other peoples of the world as against force and selfish aggression. All the peoples of the world are in effect partners in this interest, and for our own part we see very clearly that unless justice be done to others it will not be done to us. The programme of the world's peace, therefore, is our programme; and that programme, the only possible programme, as we see it, is this:

1. Open covenants of peace, openly arrived at, after which there shall be no private international understandings of any kind but diplomacy shall proceed always frankly and in the public view.
2. Absolute freedom of navigation upon the seas, outside territorial waters, alike in peace and in war, except as the seas may be closed in whole or in part by international action for the enforcement of international covenants.
3. The removal, so far as possible, of all economic barriers and the establishment of an equality of trade conditions among all the nations consenting to the peace and associating themselves for its maintenance....

conclude peace on this basis, except that the British entered a reservation about freedom of the seas, and Wilson agreed to an Anglo-French demand that the Germans be required to make reparation for damages to civilian property.

Wilson led the U.S. delegation and a large group of experts to the peace conference, which opened in Paris in January 1919. He fought heroically for his Fourteen Points against the Allied leaders—David Lloyd George of Britain, Georges Clemenceau of France, and Vittorio Orlando of Italy—who, under heavy pressure from their own constituencies, were determined to divide the territories of the vanquished and make Germany pay the full cost of the war. Wilson made a number of compromises that violated the spirit if not the letter of the Fourteen Points, including the imposition of an indefinitely large reparations bill upon Germany. Moreover, the Allies had intervened in the Russian Civil War against the dominant revolutionary socialist faction, the Bolsheviks; and Wilson had halfheartedly cooperated with

The U.S. 27th Infantry Division passing through the Victory Arch in New York City in celebration of the end of World War I, March 25, 1919. Encyclopædia Britannica, Inc.

the Allies by dispatching small numbers of troops to northern Russia, to protect military supplies against the advancing Germans, and to Siberia, mainly to keep an eye on the Japanese, who had sent a large force there. But Wilson won many more of his Fourteen Points than he lost. His greatest victories were to prevent the dismemberment of Germany in the west and further intervention in Russia and, most important, to obtain the incorporation of the Covenant of the League of Nations into the Treaty of Versailles. He was confident that the League, under American leadership, would soon rectify the injustices of the treaty.

The cover of Modern Masterpieces *magazine depicting the signing of the Treaty of Versailles in the Hall of Mirrors at the Palace of Versailles.* Hulton Archive/Getty Images

The Fight Over the Treaty and the Election of 1920

Public opinion in the United States seemed strongly in favour of quick ratification of the Treaty of Versailles when the president presented that document to the Senate for ratification on July 10, 1919, but debate continued all through the summer. Traditional isolationist sentiment was beginning to revive, and a small minority of 16 senators, irreconcilably opposed to U.S. membership in the League, vowed to oppose the treaty to the bitter end. In addition, a crucial controversy developed between the president and a majority of the Republican senators, led by Henry Cabot Lodge of Massachusetts. Lodge insisted upon adding 14 reservations to the treaty. The second reservation declared that the United States assumed no obligations under Article X of the Covenant, which guaranteed the integrity and independence of members of the League; moreover

The first session of the League of Nations, shown here, took place in Geneva in 1920. Although Pres. Woodrow Wilson was an avid proponent of the League, the United States never became a member. Hulton Archive/Getty Images

it said that the president could not use the armed forces to support the Covenant without the explicit consent of Congress.

Calling this reservation a nullification of the treaty, Wilson in September made a long speaking tour of the West to build up public support for unconditional ratification. He suffered a breakdown at the end of his tour and a serious stroke on October 2. The president's illness, which incapacitated him for several months, increased his intransigence against the Lodge reservations; with equal stubbornness, the Massachusetts senator refused to consent to any compromise. The result was failure to obtain the necessary two-thirds majority for ratification, with or without reservations, when the Senate voted on Nov. 19, 1919, and again on March 19, 1920.

Henry Cabot Lodge. Keystone/Hulton Archive/ Getty Images

Document: Henry Cabot Lodge: Reservations with Regard to the Treaty of Versailles (1919)

As the debate over the Treaty of Versailles and the proposed League of Nations ensued through the summer and autumn of 1919, Sen. Henry Cabot Lodge presented a set of reservations to the treaty that would have had the effect of circumscribing America's participation in the League. These reservations, presented on November 6, were accepted by the Senate, but two weeks later—on November 18—President Wilson wrote a letter to Sen. Gilbert Hitchcock of Nebraska urging all loyal Democrats to vote against the Lodge reservations if they wanted to preserve the treaty. The climax came on November 19, when two important votes were taken. In the first, on the question of ratification with the Lodge reservations, the loyal Democrats joined those who were irreconcilably opposed to the treaty and defeated it. In the second, on the question of ratification without reservations, the main bulk of the senators changed sides, with irreconcilables still voting against the treaty, joined this time by those, like Senator Lodge, who opposed an unqualified American commitment. The following selection comprises Senator Lodge's reservations of November 6.

Resolved (two-thirds of the senators present concurring therein), that the Senate advise and consent to the ratification of the treaty of peace with Germany concluded at Versailles on the 28th day of June, 1919, subject to the following reservations and understandings, which are hereby made a part and condition of this resolution of ratification, which ratification is not to take effect or bind the United States until the said reservations and understandings adopted by the Senate have been accepted by an exchange of notes as a part and a condition of this resolution of ratification by at least three of the four principal allied and associated powers, to wit, Great Britain, France, Italy, and Japan:

The United States so understands and construes Article 1 that in case of notice of withdrawal from the League of Nations, as provided in said article, the United States shall be the sole judge as to whether all its international obligations and all its obligations under the said Covenant have been fulfilled, and notice of withdrawal by the United States may be given by a concurrent resolution of the Congress of the United States....

Wilson had suggested that the ensuing presidential campaign and election should be a "great and solemn referendum" on the League. The Democratic candidate, James M. Cox of Ohio, fought hard to make it the leading issue, but the Republican candidate, Warren G. Harding of Ohio, was evasive on the subject, and a group of 31 leading Republican internationalists assured the country that Harding's election would be the best guarantee of U.S. membership in the League of Nations. Harding swamped Cox, and his victory ended all hopes for U.S. membership. In his inaugural Harding announced that the United States would not be entangled in European affairs; he emphasized this determination by concluding a separate peace with Germany in 1921.

A campaign button for Warren G. Harding, who won the presidential election of 1920. Blank Archives/Hulton Archive/Getty Images

The United States had emerged from the American Civil War as a booming modern industrial country. Challenged by both Americans and foreigners to play a larger role in international affairs, the U.S. government strode boldly onto the world stage at the turn of the 20th century, staking a claim to empire with acquisitions in the Caribbean and Pacific that were the fruits of the Spanish-American War. How reluctant that pursuit of empire was remains a matter of interpretation. But regardless of the motivation behind American imperialism, there is no question that by the early 20th century U.S. influence had begun to reach around the globe—from Theodore Roosevelt's declaration of his corollary to the Monroe Doctrine in Latin America and John Hay's "Open Door Policy" in China, to American involvement in Europe during World War I and Woodrow Wilson's idealistic plans in the wake of that war for a new world order founded upon rational diplomacy. By the end of the 20th century's second decade, however, the isolationism that kept the United States out of the League of Nations embodied a renewed cautiousness about involvement in world affairs, an attitude that dated from the republic's earliest days. After years of moving toward broad international engagement, American foreign policy had come full circle.

As the United States reached out to the world, the world continued to arrive on America's doorstep. It was partly in response to the needs of immigrants and their struggle to survive in the harsh environment of American industrial capitalism that progressive reform came to define the era domestically. Progressivism was a broad movement whose champions were to be found in all strata of American society: in the Oval Office and on the factory floor, in the ivory towers of academia as well as in the pulpit and in the wheatfields. Whether they were called trust-busters or suffragettes, Populists or Progressives, in government or in the private sector, these reformers endeavoured to improve the lives of rank-and-file Americans—especially those of the least well-off—by reigning in big business. Through muckraking exposés, collective activism, and groundbreaking legislation, Progressives tempered the excesses of free-market capitalism and extended the benefits and opportunities of life in the United States beyond the gilded palaces of privilege. As America entered the 1920s, it was a more equitable society, but in the decades that followed its evolving economy, culture, and society would be tested by the cataclysm of the Great Depression and another world war.

APPENDICES (DOCUMENTS)

ALBERT SHAW: THE BLOWING UP OF THE *MAINE* (1898)

Source: *American Monthly Review of Reviews*, April 1898: "The Progress of the World."

The weeks that have elapsed since that fatal event of February 15th have been making history in a manner highly creditable to the American government and to our citizenship. Captain Sigsbee, the commander of the *Maine*, had promptly telegraphed his desire that judgment should be suspended until investigation had been made. The investigation was set on foot at once, and 75 million Americans have accordingly suspended judgment in the face of a great provocation. For it must be remembered that to suppose the destruction of the *Maine* an ordinary accident and not due to any external agency or hostile intent was, under all the circumstances, to set completely at defiance the law of probabilities.

It is not true that battleships are in the habit of blowing themselves up. When all the environing facts were taken into consideration, it was just about as probable that the *Maine* had been blown up by spontaneous combustion or by some accident in which no hostile motive was concerned, as that the reported assassination of President Barrios of Guatemala, a few days previously, had really been a suicide....

It has been known perfectly well that Spanish hatred might at any time manifest itself by attempts upon the life of the American representative at Havana, Consul General Fitzhugh Lee. This danger was felt especially at the time of the Havana riots in January, and it seems to have had something to do with the sending of the *Maine* to Havana Harbor. The Spaniards themselves, however, looked upon the sending of the *Maine* as a further aggravation of the long series of their just grievances against the United States. They regarded the presence of the *Maine* at Havana as a menace to Spanish sovereignty in the island and as an encouragement to the insurgents. A powerful American fleet lay at Key West and the Dry Tortugas, with steam up ready to follow the *Maine* to the harbor of Havana on a few hours' notice. All this was intensely hateful to the Spaniards, and particularly to the Army officers at Havana who had sympathized with General Weyler's policy and who justly regarded General Weyler's recall to Spain as due to the demand of President McKinley. The American pretense that the *Maine* was making a visit of courtesy seemed to these Spaniards a further example of Anglo-Saxon hypocrisy.

That this intense bitterness against the presence of the *Maine* was felt among the military and official class in Havana was perfectly well known to Captain Sigsbee, his staff, and all his crew; and they were not unaware of the rumors and threats that means would be found to destroy the American ship. It was, furthermore, very generally supposed that the Spanish preparation for the defense of Havana had included mines and torpedoes in the harbor. At the time when the *Maine* went to Havana, it was a notorious fact that the relations between Spain and the United States were so strained that war was regarded as almost inevitable. If war had actually been declared while the *Maine* was at Havana, it is not likely that the Spanish would have permitted the ship's departure without an effort to do her harm.

The Spanish harbor is now and it has been for a good while past under absolute military control; and the American warship, believed by the Spanish authorities to be at Havana with only half-cloaked hostile designs, was obliged to accept the anchorage that was assigned by those very authorities. In view of the strained situation and of the Spanish feeling that no magnanimity is due on Spain's part toward the United States, it is not in the least difficult to believe that the harbor authorities would have anchored the *Maine* at a spot where, in case of the outbreak of war, the submarine harbor defenses might be effectively used against so formidable an enemy.

To understand the situation completely, it must not be forgotten that the Spanish government at first made objection against the *Maine*'s intended visit to Havana and, in consenting, merely yielded to a necessity that was forced upon it. All Spaniards regarded the sending of the *Maine* to Havana as really a treacherous act on the part of the United States, and most of them would have deemed it merely a safe and reasonable precautionary measure to anchor her in the vicinity of a submarine mine. Doubtless these suggestions will be read by more than one person who will receive them with entire skepticism. But such readers will not have been familiar with what has been going on in the matter of the Cuban rebellion, or else they will be lacking in memories of good carrying power.

The great majority of the intelligent people of the United States could not, from the first, avoid perceiving that what we may call the self-destruction theory was extremely improbable; while what we may term the assassination theory was in keeping with all the circumstances. Nevertheless, although the probability of guilt was so overwhelming, the American people saw the fairness and the necessity of suspending judgment until proof had been substituted for mere probability. And there was in no part of the country any disposition to take snap judgment or to act precipitately. No other such spectacle of national forbearance has been witnessed in our times.

Unquestionably, the whole community has been intensely eager for news; and it is perhaps true that certain newspapers, which have devoted themselves for a month or more to criticizing the sensational press, might as well have been occupied in a more energetic effort to supply their readers with information. The fact is that the so-called war extras, which for many days were issued from certain newspaper offices at the rate of a dozen or more a day, have not seemed to communicate their hysteria to any considerable number of the American people, East or West, North or South, so far as our observation goes.

The situation has simply been one of a very absorbing and profound interest, while the suspense has been very trying to the nerves. The possibility that our country might soon be engaged in war with a foreign power has been a pre-occupying thought not to be dismissed for a single hour. The whole country has known that a fateful investigation was in progress in Havana Harbor; that coast-defense work was being pushed all along our seaboard; that in all the ship-yards, public and private, government work was being prosecuted with double or quadruple forces of men, working by night as well as by day; that ammuni-tion factories, iron and steel plants, and every other establishment capable of furnishing any kind of military or naval supplies were receiving orders from the government and were working to the full extent of their capacity; that plans were being made for fitting out mer-chant ships as auxiliary cruisers; that our naval representatives were nego-tiating abroad for additional warships; that new regiments of artillerymen were being enlisted for the big guns on the seaboard; that naval recruits were being mustered in to man newly commissioned

ships; that the railroads were preparing by order of the War Department to bring the little United States Army from west-ern and northern posts to convenient southern centers; and that while we were making these preparations Spain on her part was trying to raise money to buy ships and to secure allies. All these matters, and many others related to them, have within these past weeks made an immense opportunity for test-ing the news gathering resources of the American press....

When, therefore, on March 8, the House of Representatives unanimously voted to place $50 million at the unquali-fied disposal of President McKinley as an emergency fund for the national defense—this action being followed by an equally unanimous vote of the Senate the next day—it was naturally taken for granted all over the country that the situation was believed by the President to be extremely critical. The continued delay of the Board of Inquiry—which had been oscillating between Havana and Key West, conducting its proceed-ings in secret and mantaining absolute reticence—had naturally served to con-firm the belief that its report would show foul play; and it appeared that the President was basing his great prepa-rations of war, in part at least, upon his advance knowledge of the evidence secured by the commission. The una-nimity of Congress in support of the President created an excellent impres-sion abroad. Fifty million is a very large sum to place in the hands of one man.

It might have been supposed that there would have been members in both houses who would have insisted upon the appropriation of this money for specific purposes. That not a single man was found to make objection showed a very great capacity for united action in a time of emergency. It also showed, of course, how great is the confidence that Congress and the American people repose in the honor, wisdom, and public spirit of their Presidents. At the time of the Venezuela incident, Congress in similar manner, came unanimously to the support of President Cleveland. In that case, however, there was not the remotest possibility of war; and the episode was merely a diplomatic one in which it was deemed important to show that our government could rely absolutely upon the whole support of the people. The South on all such recent occasions has been foremost in expressions of patriotism.

The vote of $50 million, although an extraordinary measure justified only by the imminent danger of war, was clearly an act that no peace-loving man could reasonably criticize; for preparation is often the means by which conflict is avoided. A larger Navy was in any case greatly desirable for our country, with its long seaboard on the Atlantic and the Pacific and its vast commerce; while the better fortification of our principal ports was an urgent necessity. Since the preparations that have been made so hurriedly during the past few weeks have been of a defensive nature, and since they have been carried out upon lines which had

been duly considered in advance, they will have permanent value, and there will have been involved a very small percentage of waste. If Congress had been wise enough in the past three or four years to lay down more warships in our own yards, it would not have been necessary to contribute millions to foreign shipbuilders.

No part of the $50 million will be squandered by the administration; but it is to be regretted that this emergency fund had not been already expended during the five preceding years by more liberal appropriations for coast defense and naval construction. The great shipyards of the United States, both public and private, are now at the point where, with a sufficient amount of regular work to do, they would speedily be able to compete on equal terms with the best shipbuilding plants of Europe. Iron and steel supplies are now much cheaper in the United States than anywhere else, and it is only the relatively small amount of shipbuilding that has been demanded by our government that has made it more expensive to build a war vessel here than elsewhere.

In a time of real emergency, however, the resources of the United States would prove themselves great enough to supply our own people and the whole world besides. The quickness and inventiveness of American mechanics, engineers, and manufacturers have no parallel in Europe. On a year's notice the United States might undertake to cope even-handed with either the Dual or the Triple Alliance—although we have now only the nucleus of an army and the beginning of a navy, while the European powers have made war preparation their principal business for a whole generation. It is to be suspected that one reason why the American people have bought the newspapers so eagerly during the past weeks is to be found in the satisfaction they have taken in learning how a strictly peaceful nation like ours could if necessary reverse the process of beating swords into plowshares.

It is true, for example, that we have built only a few torpedo boats and only a few vessels of the type known as destroyers; but we have discovered that about a hundred very rich Americans had been amusing themselves within the past few years by building or buying splendid oceangoing, steel-built steam yachts of high speed and stanch qualities, capable of being quickly transformed into naval dispatch boats or armored and fitted with torpedo tubes. Probably not a single private Spanish citizen could turn over to his government such a vessel as the magnificent Goelet yacht, the *Mayflower*, which was secured by our Navy Department on March 16; not to mention scores of other private steam yachts of great size and strength that wealthy American citizens are ready to offer if needed.

It is the prevailing opinion nowadays, it is true, that nothing is to be relied upon in naval war but huge battleships, which take from two to three or four years to build. But if a great war were forced upon us suddenly, it is altogether probable that American ingenuity would devise something wholly new in the way of a marine engine of war, just as American ingenuity improvised the first modern ironclads. We have already in our Navy a dynamite cruiser, the *Vesuvius*, which in actual warfare might prove more dangerous than a half dozen of the greatest battleships of the European navies. There has just been completed, moreover, and offered to our government, a submarine boat, the *Holland*, which seems to be capable of moving rapidly for several miles so completely submerged as to offer no target for an enemy; and it may well be that the torpedoes discharged from an insignificant little vessel capable of swimming below the surface like a fish might prove as fatal to the battleships of an enemy as the alleged mine in the harbor of Havana was fatal to our battleship the *Maine*.

Nowadays, warfare is largely a matter of science and invention; and since a country where the arts of peace flourish and prosper is most favorable to the general advance of science and invention, we stumble upon the paradox that the successful pursuit of peace is after all the best preparation for war. Another way to put it is to say that modern warfare has become a matter of machinery, and that the most highly developed mechanical and industrial nation will by virtue of such development be most formidable in war.

This is a situation that the Spaniards in general are evidently quite unable to comprehend. Their ideas are altogether medieval. They believe themselves to be a highly chivalrous and militant people, and that the people of the United States are really in great terror of Spanish prowess. They think that Spain could make as easy work of invading the United States as Japan made of invading China. Their point of view is altogether theatrical and unrelated to modern facts.

A country like ours, capable of supplying the whole world with electrical motors, mining machinery, locomotive engines, steel rails, and the structural material for modern steel bridges and "skyscrapers," not to mention bicycles and sewing machines, is equally capable of building, arming, and operating an unlimited number of ships of every type, and of employing every conceivable mechanical device for purposes of national defense. In the long run, therefore, even if our preliminary preparations had been of the scantiest character, we should be able to give a good account of ourselves in warfare....

Quite regardless of the responsibilities for the *Maine* incident, it is apparently true that the great majority of the American people are hoping that President McKinley will promptly utilize the occasion to secure the complete pacification and independence of Cuba. There are a few people in the United States—we should not like to believe that more than 100 could be found out of a population of 75 million—who believe that the United States ought to join hands with Spain in forcing the Cuban insurgents to lay down their arms and to accept Spanish sovereignty as a permanent condition under the promise of practical home rule. It needs no argument, of course, to convince the American people that such a proposal reaches the lowest depths of infamy. It is much worse than the proposition made by a few people in Europe last year that the victorious Turks should have the countenance and support of the great nations of Europe in making Greece a part of the Turkish empire. For the Turks had fairly conquered the Greeks; and if Europe had kept hands off, Greece would have been reduced very quickly to the position of an Ottoman province.

But in Cuba it is otherwise. The insurgents, with no outside help, have held their own for more than three years, and Spain is unable to conquer them. The people of the United States do not intend to help Spain hold Cuba. On the contrary, they are now ready, in one way or in another, to help the Cubans drive Spain out of the Western Hemisphere. If the occasion goes past and we allow this Cuban struggle to run on indefinitely, the American people will have lost several degrees of self-respect and will certainly not have gained anything in the opinion of mankind.

CHARLES DENBY: THE EVIDENT FITNESS OF KEEPING THE PHILIPPINES (1898)

Source: *Forum*, November 1898: "Shall We Keep the Philippines?"

Dewey's victory has changed our attitude before the world. We took no part in international questions. We had no standing in the councils of the nations. We were a *quantité négligeable*. So far did the idea that we ought to take no part in foreign questions extend that some of my colleagues at Peking, when I undertook to make peace for China and Japan, deprecated any intervention whatever of the United States in the affairs of the Far East!

The position of absolute indifference to what is happening in the world is difficult of maintenance; and when it is maintained it is humiliating.

I recognize the existence of a national sentiment in accordance with the supposed teaching of Washington's Farewell Address, which is against the acquisition of foreign territory; but the world has moved and circumstances are changed. We have become a great people. We have a great commerce to take care of. We have to compete with the commercial nations of the world in far-distant markets. Commerce, not politics, is king. The manufacturer and the merchant dictate to diplomacy and control elections. The art of arts is the extension of commercial relations—in plain language, the selling of native products and manufactured goods.

I learned what I know of diplomacy in a severe school. I found among my colleagues not the least hesitation in proposing to their respective governments to do anything which was supposed to be conducive to their interests. There can be no other rule for the government of all persons who are charged with the conduct of affairs than the promotion of the welfare of their respective countries. If it be ascertained or believed that the acquisition of the Philippines would be of advantage of this country then mere sentiment must give way to actual benefit.

It is well known that prophecies of evil have preceded every acquisition we ever made, from the Louisiana Purchase to that of Alaska; and, judging by the results of the various annexations, these prophecies have been misleading.

There is no reason whatever why we cannot administer the Philippines in a manner satisfactory to their people as well as to ourselves. We have recently annexed the Hawaiian Islands. They lie at what are called the "crossroads of the North Pacific." They are near the center of the great lines of commerce from the East to the West. There is little dissent from the policy of their annexation. It is not imagined that their peaceful people will require a great army to control them.

If it could be ascertained today that no army would be necessary, or that a small body of troops at most would be sufficient, to safeguard the Philippines, opposition to their annexation would be greatly diminished. It is simply the dread of a large standing army that causes the body of the people who oppose annexation to withhold their approval. I do not believe that a large army will be necessary in the Philippines; and I am sure that, imitating the policy of England in East India, native troops would serve all purposes.

We have the right as conquerors to hold the Philippines. We have the right to hold them as part payment of a war indemnity. This policy may be characterized as unjust to Spain; but it is the result of the fortunes of war. All nations recognize that the conqueror may dictate the terms of peace. The first answer I received to a telegram sent by me, asking on the part of China that peace negotiations should be commenced and offering to concede the independence of Korea and to pay a reasonable war indemnity, was: "Japan is willing to enter on peace negotiations; but she will dictate the terms."

I am in favor of holding the Philippines because I cannot conceive of any alternative to our doing so, except the seizure of territory in China; and I prefer to hold them rather than to oppress further the helpless government and people of China. I want China to preserve her autonomy, to become great and prosperous; and I want these results, not for the interests of China but for our interests. I am not the agent or attorney of China; and, as an American, I do not look to the promotion of China's interests, or Spain's, or any other country's, but simply of our own.

The whole world sees in China a splendid market for our native products—our timber, our locomotives, our rails, our coal oil, our sheetings, our mining plants, and numberless other articles. We are closer to her than any other commercial country except Japan. There is before us a boundless future which will make the Pacific more important to us than the Atlantic. San Francisco, Seattle, and Tacoma are in their infancy. They are destined to rival New York, Chicago, and Philadelphia.

If we give up the Philippines, we throw away the splendid opportunity to assert our influence in the Far East. We do this deliberately; and the world will laugh at us. Why did we take Manila? Why did we send 20,000 troops to Luzon? Did we do so to emulate the French king who marched his men up the hill and down again? There was no purpose in the conquest of Manila unless we intended to hold it.

The Philippines are a foothold for us in the Far East. Their possession gives us standing and influence. It gives us also valuable trade both in exports and imports.

Should we surrender the Philippines, what will become of them? Will Spain ever conquer the insurgents, and, should she do so, will she retain the islands? To her they will be valueless; and if she sells them to any continental power she will, by that act, light the torches of war.

It is perfectly certain, I think, that England will not stand by and see any other European power take the Philippines. They are on the line to Australia and India. England has stood by and seen Germany, Russia, and France seize portions of China. There is not an Englishman nor an American in the Far East who approves her policy. The taking of the Philippines by any European power other than England would create an explosion in the latter country, and, if unresisted, would lead to the destruction of the ministry and, perhaps, the throne.

By holding the Philippines we avert the partition of China, and we postpone at least a general European war.

There is, perhaps, no such thing as manifest destiny; but there is an evident fitness in the happening of events and a logical result of human action.

Dewey's victory is an epoch in the affairs of the Far East. We hold our heads higher. We are coming to our own. We are stretching out our hands for what nature meant should be ours. We are taking our proper rank among the nations of the world. We are after markets, the greatest markets now existing in the world. Along with these markets will go our beneficent institutions, and humanity will bless us.

WILLIAM JENNINGS BRYAN: THE PARALYZING INFLUENCE OF IMPERIALISM (1900)

Source: *Official Proceedings of the Democratic National Convention Held in Kansas City, Mo., July 4, 5, and 6, 1900,* Chicago, 1900, pp. 205–227.

If it is right for the United States to hold the Philippine Islands permanently and imitate European empires in the government of colonies, the Republican Party ought to state its position and defend it, but it must expect the subject races to protest against such a policy and to resist to the extent of their ability.

The Filipinos do not need any encouragement from Americans now living. Our whole history has been an encouragement, not only to the Filipinos but to all who are denied a voice in their own government. If the Republicans are prepared to censure all who have used language calculated to make the Filipinos hate foreign domination, let them condemn the speech of Patrick Henry. When he uttered that passionate appeal, "Give me liberty or give me death," he expressed a sentiment which still echoes in the hearts of men.

Let them censure Jefferson; of all the statesmen of history none have used words so offensive to those who would hold their fellows in political bondage. Let them censure Washington, who declared that the colonists must choose between liberty and slavery. Or, if the statute of limitations has run against the sins of Henry and Jefferson and Washington, let them censure Lincoln, whose Gettysburg speech will be quoted in defense of popular government when the present advocates of force and conquest are forgotten.

Someone has said that a truth once spoken can never be recalled. It goes on and on, and no one can set a limit to its ever widening influence. But if it were possible to obliterate every word written or spoken in defense of the principles set forth in the Declaration of Independence, a war of conquest would still leave its legacy of perpetual hatred, for it was God Himself who placed in every human heart the love of liberty. He never made a race of people so low in the scale of civilization or intelligence that it would welcome a foreign master.

Those who would have this nation enter upon a career of empire must consider not only the effect of imperialism on the Filipinos but they must also calculate its effects upon our own nation. We cannot repudiate the principle of self-government in the Philippines without weakening that principle here.

Lincoln said that the safety of this nation was not in its fleets, its armies, its forts, but in the spirit which prizes liberty as the heritage of all men, in all lands, everywhere, and he warned his countrymen that they could not destroy this spirit without planting the seeds of despotism at their own doors.

Even now we are beginning to see the paralyzing influence of imperialism. Heretofore this nation has been prompt to express its sympathy with those who were fighting for civil liberty. While our sphere of activity has been limited to the Western Hemisphere, our sympathies have not been bounded by the seas. We have felt it due to ourselves and to the world, as well as to those who were struggling for the right to govern themselves, to proclaim the interest which our people have, from the date of their own independence, felt in every contest between human rights and arbitrary power....

A colonial policy means that we shall send to the Philippine Islands a few traders, a few taskmasters, and a few officeholders, and an army large enough to support the authority of a small fraction of the people while they rule the natives.

If we have an imperial policy we must have a great standing army as its natural and necessary complement.

The spirit which will justify the forcible annexation of the Philippine Islands will justify the seizure of other islands and the domination of other people, and with wars of conquest we can expect a certain, if not rapid, growth of our military establishment.

That a large permanent increase in our regular army is intended by Republican leaders is not a matter of conjecture but a matter of fact. In his message of Dec. 5, 1898, the President asked for authority to increase the standing army to 100,000. In 1896 the army contained about 25,000. Within two years the President asked for four times that many, and a Republican House of Representatives complied with the request after the Spanish treaty had been signed, and when no country was at war with the United States.

If such an army is demanded when an imperial policy is contemplated but not openly avowed, what may be expected if the people encourage the Republican Party by endorsing its policy at the polls?

A large standing army is not only a pecuniary burden to the people and, if accompanied by compulsory service, a constant source of irritation but it is even a menace to a republican form of government. The army is the personification of force, and militarism will inevitably change the ideals of the people and turn the thoughts of our young men from the arts of peace to the science of war. The government which relies for its defense upon its citizens is more likely to be just than one which has at call a large body of professional soldiers.

A small standing army and a well-equipped and well-disciplined state militia are sufficient at ordinary times, and in an emergency the nation should in the future as in the past place its dependence upon the volunteers who come from all occupations at their country's call and return to productive labor when their services are no longer required—men who fight when the country needs fighters and work when the country needs workers....

The Republican platform promises that some measure of self-government is to be given the Filipinos by law; but even this pledge is not fulfilled. Nearly sixteen months elapsed after the ratification of the treaty before the adjournment of Congress last June and yet no law was passed dealing with the Philippine situation. The will of the President has been the only law in the Philippine Islands wherever the American authority extends.

Why does the Republican Party hesitate to legislate upon the Philippine question? Because a law would disclose the radical departure from history and precedent contemplated by those who control the Republican Party. The storm of protest which greeted the Puerto Rican bill was an indication of what may be expected when the American people are brought face to face with legislation upon this subject.

If the Puerto Ricans, who welcomed annexation, are to be denied the guarantees of our Constitution, what is to be the lot of the Filipinos, who resisted our authority? If secret influences could compel a disregard of our plain duty toward friendly people living near our shores, what treatment will those same influences provide for unfriendly people 7,000 miles away? If, in this country where the people have a right to vote, Republican leaders dare not take the side of the people against the great monopolies which have grown up within the last few years, how can they be trusted to protect the Filipinos from the corporations which are waiting to exploit the islands?

Is the sunlight of full citizenship to be enjoyed by the people of the United States and the twilight of semi-citizenship endured by the people of Puerto Rico, while the thick darkness of perpetual vassalage covers the Philippines? The Puerto Rico tariff law asserts the doctrine that the operation of the Constitution is confined to the forty-five states.

The Democratic Party disputes this doctrine and denounces it as repugnant to both the letter and spirit of our organic law. There is no place in our system of government for the deposit of arbitrary and irresistible power. That the leaders of a great party should claim for any President or Congress the right to treat millions of people as mere "possessions" and deal with them unrestrained by the Constitution or the Bill of Rights shows how far we have already departed from the ancient landmarks and indicates what may be expected if this nation deliberately enters upon a career of empire.

The territorial form of government is temporary and preparatory, and the chief security a citizen of a territory has is found in the fact that he enjoys the same constitutional guarantees and is subject to the same general laws as the citizen of a state. Take away this security and his rights will be violated and his interests sacrificed at the demand of those who have political influence. This is the evil of the colonial system, no matter by what nation it is applied.

What is our title to the Philippine Islands? Do we hold them by treaty or by conquest? Did we buy them or did we take them? Did we purchase the people? If not, how did we secure title to them? Were they thrown in with the land? Will the Republicans say that inanimate earth has value but that when that earth is molded by the Divine Hand and stamped with the likeness of the Creator it becomes a fixture and passes with the soil? If governments derive their just powers from the consent of the governed, it is impossible to secure title to people, either by force or by purchase.

We could extinguish Spain's title by treaty, but if we hold title we must hold it by some method consistent with our ideas of government. When we made allies of the Filipinos and armed them to fight against Spain, we disputed Spain's title. If we buy Spain's title, we are not innocent purchasers. There can be no doubt that we accepted and utilized the services of the Filipinos and that when we did so we had full knowledge that they were fighting for their own independence; and I submit that history furnishes no example of turpitude baser than ours

if we now substitute our yoke for the Spanish yoke....

Some argue that American rule in the Philippine Islands will result in the better education of the Filipinos. Be not deceived. If we expect to maintain a colonial policy, we shall not find it to our advantage to educate the people. The educated Filipinos are now in revolt against us, and the most ignorant ones have made the least resistance to our domination. If we are to govern them without their consent and give them no voice in determining the taxes which they must pay, we dare not educate them lest they learn to read the Declaration of Independence and the Constitution of the United States and mock us for our inconsistency.

The principal arguments, however, advanced by those who enter upon a defense of imperialism are:

First, that we must improve the present opportunity to become a world power and enter into international politics.

Second, that our commercial interests in the Philippine Islands and in the Orient make it necessary for us to hold the islands permanently.

Third, that the spread of the Christian religion will be facilitated by a colonial policy.

Fourth, that there is no honorable retreat from the position which the nation has taken.

The first argument is addressed to the nation's pride and the second to the nation's pocketbook. The third is intended for the church member and the fourth for the partisan.

It is sufficient answer to the first argument to say that for more than a century this nation has been a world power. For ten decades it has been the most potent influence in the world. Not only has it been a world power but it has done more to affect the policies of the human race than all the other nations of the world combined. Because our Declaration of Independence was promulgated, others have been promulgated. Because the patriots of 1776 fought for liberty, others have fought for it. Because our Constitution was adopted, other constitutions have been adopted.

The growth of the principle of self-government, planted on American soil, has been the overshadowing political fact of the 19th century. It has made this nation conspicuous among the nations and given it a place in history such as no other nation has ever enjoyed. Nothing has been able to check the onward march of this idea. I am not willing that this nation shall cast aside the omnipotent weapon of truth to seize again the weapons of physical warfare. I would not exchange the glory of this republic for the glory of all the empires that have risen and fallen since time began.

The permanent chairman of the last Republican National Convention presented the pecuniary argument in all its baldness when he said:

We make no hypocritical pretense of being interested in the Philippines solely on account of others. While we regard the welfare of those people as a sacred trust, we regard the welfare of the American people first. We see our duty to ourselves as well as to others. We believe in trade expansion. By every legitimate means within the province of government and constitution we mean to stimulate the expansion of our trade and open new markets.

This is the commercial argument. It is based upon the theory that war can be rightly waged for pecuniary advantage and that it is profitable to purchase trade by force and violence. Franklin denied both of these propositions. When Lord Howe asserted that the acts of Parliament which brought on the Revolution were necessary to prevent American trade from passing into foreign channels, Franklin replied:

To me it seems that neither the obtaining nor retaining of any trade, howsoever valuable, is an object for which men may justly spill each other's blood; that the true and sure means of extending and securing commerce are the goodness and cheapness of commodities, and that the profits of no trade can ever be equal to the expense of compelling it and holding it by fleets and armies. I consider this war against us, therefore, as both unjust and unwise.

I place the philosophy of Franklin against the sordid doctrine of those who would put a price upon the head of an American soldier and justify a war of conquest upon the ground that it will pay. The Democratic Party is in favor of the expansion of trade. It would extend our trade by every legitimate and peaceful means; but it is not willing to make merchandise of human blood.

But a war of conquest is as unwise as it is unrighteous. A harbor and coaling station in the Philippines would answer every trade and military necessity and such a concession could have been secured at any time without difficulty. It is not necessary to own people in order to trade with them. We carry on trade today with every part of the world, and our commerce has expanded more rapidly than the commerce of any European empire. We do not own Japan or China, but we trade with their people. We have not absorbed the republics of Central and South America, but we trade with them. Trade cannot be permanently profitable unless it is voluntary.

When trade is secured by force, the cost of securing it and retaining it must be taken out of the profits, and the profits are never large enough to cover the expense. Such a system would never be defended but for the fact that the expense is borne by all the people while the profits are enjoyed by a few.

Imperialism would be profitable to the Army contractors; it would be profitable to the shipowners, who would carry live soldiers to the Philippines and bring dead soldiers back; it would be profitable to those who would seize upon the franchises, and it would be profitable to the officials whose salaries would be fixed here and paid over there; but to the farmer, to the laboring man, and to the vast majority of those engaged in other occupations, it would bring expenditure without return and risk without reward.

Farmers and laboring men have, as a rule, small incomes, and, under systems which place the tax upon consumption, pay much more than their fair share of the expenses of government. Thus the very people who receive least benefit from imperialism will be injured most by the military burdens which accompany it. In addition to the evils which he and the former share in common, the laboring man will be the first to suffer if Oriental subjects seek work in the United States; the first to suffer if American capital leaves our shores to employ Oriental labor in the Philippines to supply the trade of China and Japan; the first to suffer from the violence which the military spirit arouses, and the first to suffer when the methods of imperialism are applied to our own government. It is not strange, therefore, that the labor organizations have been quick to note the approach of these dangers and prompt to protest against both militarism and imperialism.

The pecuniary argument, though more effective with certain classes, is not likely to be used so often or presented with so much enthusiasm as the religious argument. If what has been termed the "gunpowder gospel" were urged against the Filipinos only, it would be a suffi-cient answer to say that a majority of the Filipinos are now members of one branch of the Christian Church; but the principle involved is one of much wider application and challenges serious consideration.

The religious argument varies in positiveness from a passive belief that Providence delivered the Filipinos into our hands for their good and our glory to the exultation of the minister who said that we ought to "thrash the natives (Filipinos) until they understand who we are," and that "every bullet sent, every cannon shot, and every flag waved means righteousness."

We cannot approve of this doctrine in one place unless we are willing to apply it everywhere. If there is poison in the blood of the hand, it will ultimately reach the heart. It is equally true that forcible Christianity, if planted under the American flag in the far-away Orient, will sooner or later be transplanted upon American soil....

The argument made by some that it was unfortunate for the nation that it had anything to do with the Philippine Islands, but that the naval victory at Manila made the permanent acquisi-tion of those islands necessary, is also unsound. We won a naval victory at Santiago, but that did not compel us to hold Cuba.

The shedding of American blood in the Philippine Islands does not make it imperative that we should retain posses-sion forever; American blood was shed at San Juan Hill and El Caney, and yet the President has promised the Cubans inde-pendence. The fact that the American flag floats over Manila does not compel us to exercise perpetual sovereignty over the islands; the American flag waves over Havana today, but the President has promised to haul it down when the flag of the Cuban republic is ready to rise in its place. Better a thousand times that our flag in the Orient give way to a flag representing the idea of self-government than that the flag of this republic should become the flag of an empire.

There is an easy, honest, honorable solution of the Philippine question. It is set forth in the Democratic platform and it is submitted with confidence to the American people. This plan I unreserv-edly endorse. If elected, I will convene Congress in extraordinary session as soon as inaugurated and recommend an immediate declaration of the nation's purpose: first, to establish a stable form of government in the Philippine Islands, just as we are now establishing a stable form of government in Cuba; second, to give independence to the Cubans; third, to protect the Filipinos from outside interference while they work out their destiny, just as we have protected the republics of Central and South America, and are, by the Monroe Doctrine, pledged to protect Cuba.

A European protectorate often results in the plundering of the ward by the guardian. An American protectorate gives to the nation protected the advan-tage of our strength without making it the victim of our greed. For three-quarters of a century the Monroe Doctrine has been a shield to neighboring republics and yet it has imposed no pecuniary burden upon us. After the Filipinos had aided us in the war against Spain, we could not honorably turn them over to their former masters; we could not leave them to be the victims of the ambitious designs of European nations, and since we do not desire to make them a part of us or to hold them as subjects, we propose the only alternative, namely, to give them independence and guard them against molestation from without.

When our opponents are unable to defend their position by argument, they fall back upon the assertion that it is destiny and insist that we must submit to it no matter how much it violates our moral precepts and our principles of government. This is a complacent philosophy. It obliterates the distinction between right and wrong and makes individuals and nations the helpless victims of circumstances. Destiny is the subterfuge of the invertebrate, who, lacking the courage to oppose error, seeks some plausible excuse for supporting it. Washington said that the destiny of the republican form of government was deeply, if not finally, staked on the experiment entrusted to the American people.

How different Washington's definition of destiny from the Republican definition! The Republicans say that this nation is in the hands of destiny; Washington believed that not only the destiny of our own nation but the destiny of the republican form

of government throughout the world was entrusted to American hands. Immeasurable responsibility!

The destiny of this republic is in the hands of its own people, and upon the success of the experiment here rests the hope of humanity. No exterior force can disturb this republic, and no foreign influence should be permitted to change its course. What the future has in store for this nation no one has authority to declare, but each individual has his own idea of the nation's mission, and he owes it to his country as well as to himself to contribute as best he may to the fulfillment of that mission.

Mr. Chairman and Gentlemen of the Committee, I can never fully discharge the debt of gratitude which I owe to my countrymen for the honors which they have so generously bestowed upon me; but, sirs, whether it be my lot to occupy the high office for which the convention has named me or to spend the remainder of my days in private life, it shall be my constant ambition and my controlling purpose to aid in realizing the high ideals of those whose wisdom and courage and sacrifices brought this republic into existence.

I can conceive of a national destiny surpassing the glories of the present and the past—a destiny which meets the responsibilities of today and measures up to the possibilities of the future. Behold a republic, resting securely upon the foundation stones quarried by revolutionary patriots from the mountain of eternal truth—a republic applying in practice and proclaiming to the world the self-evident proposition that all men are created equal; that they are endowed with inalienable rights; that governments are instituted among men to secure these rights, and that governments derive their just powers from the consent of the governed.

Behold a republic in which civil and religious liberty stimulate all to earnest endeavor and in which the law restrains every hand uplifted for a neighbor's injury—a republic in which every citizen is a sovereign, but in which no one cares to wear a crown. Behold a republic standing erect while empires all around are bowed beneath the weight of their own armaments—a republic whose flag is loved while other flags are only feared. Behold a republic increasing in population, in wealth, in strength, and in influence, solving the problems of civilization and hastening the coming of an universal brotherhood—a republic which shakes thrones and dissolves aristocracies by its silent example and gives light and inspiration to those who sit in darkness. Behold a republic gradually but surely becoming a supreme moral factor in the world's progress and the accepted arbiter of the world's disputes—a republic whose history, like the path of the just, "is as the shining light that shineth more and more unto the perfect day."

JOHN HAY: THE OPEN DOOR POLICY (1899)

Source: [Senate Foreign Relations Committee] *Treaties, Conventions,*

International Acts, Protocols and Agreements between the United States of America and other Powers 1776-1909, William M. Malloy, ed., Washington, 1910, Vol. I, pp. 246–247.

In 1899 trade with China amounted to only about two percent of the total U.S. trade. Nevertheless, the American government was concerned that China's independence be preserved in the hope that trade might increase. Great Britain, with a much greater stake in China, shared this concern and prodded the United States, behind the scenes, into declaring an "Open Door Policy" toward China. British interests were served when, on September 6, 1899, Secretary of State John Hay, having informed a few Englishmen of his intention, sent the following "circular letter" to Germany, Russia, and England. Although the provisions of the policy were rather narrow, the letter was followed up the next year by a broader guarantee of China's territorial integrity.

At the time when the government of the United States was informed by that of Germany that it had leased from His Majesty the Emperor of China the port of Kiaochao and the adjacent territory in the province of Shantung, assurances were given to the ambassador of the United States at Berlin by the Imperial German minister for foreign affairs that the rights and privileges insured by treaties with China to citizens of the United States would not thereby suffer or be in anywise impaired within the area over which Germany had thus obtained control.

More recently, however, the British government recognized by a formal agreement with Germany the exclusive right of the latter country to enjoy in said leased area and the contiguous "sphere of influence or interest" certain privileges, more especially those relating to railroads and mining enterprises; but, as the exact nature and extent of the rights thus recognized have not been clearly defined, it is possible that serious conflicts of interest may at any time arise, not only between British and German subjects within said area but that the interests of our citizens may also be jeopardized thereby.

Earnestly desirous to remove any cause of irritation and to insure at the same time to the commerce of all nations in China the undoubted benefits which should accrue from a formal recognition by the various powers claiming "spheres of interest" that they shall enjoy perfect equality of treatment for their commerce and navigation within such "spheres," the government of the United States would be pleased to see His German Majesty's government give formal assurances and lend its cooperation in securing like assurances from the other interested powers that each within its respective sphere of whatever influence:

First, will in no way interfere with any treaty port or any vested interest within any so-called sphere of interest or leased territory it may have in China.

Second, that the Chinese treaty tariff of the time being shall apply to all merchandise landed or shipped to all such ports as are within said "sphere of interest" (unless they be "free ports"), no matter to what nationality it may belong, and that duties so leviable shall be collected by the Chinese government.

Third, that it will levy no higher harbor dues on vessels of another nationality frequenting any port in such "sphere" than shall be levied on vessels of its own nationality, and no higher railroad charges over lines built, controlled, or operated within its "sphere" on merchandise belonging to citizens or subjects of other nationalities transported through such "sphere" than shall be levied on similar merchandise belonging to its own nationals transported over equal distances.

The liberal policy pursued by His Imperial German Majesty in declaring Kiao-chao a free port and in aiding the Chinese government in the establishment there of a customhouse are so clearly in line with the proposition which this government is anxious to see recognized that it entertains the strongest hope that Germany will give its acceptance and hearty support.

The recent ukase of His Majesty the Emperor of Russia declaring the port of Talienwan open, during the whole of the lease under which it is held from China, to the merchant ships of all nations, coupled with the categorical assurances made to this government by His Imperial Majesty's representative at this capital at the time, and since repeated to me by the present Russian ambassador, seem to insure the support of the emperor to the proposed measure. Our ambassador at the Court of St. Petersburg has, in consequence, been instructed to submit it to the Russian government and to request their early consideration of it. A copy of my instruction on the subject to Mr. Tower is herewith enclosed for your confidential information.

The commercial interests of Great Britain and Japan will be so clearly served by the desired declaration of intentions, and the views of the governments of these countries as to the desirability of the adoption of measures insuring the benefits of equality of treatment of all foreign trade throughout China are so similar to those entertained by the United States, that their acceptance of the propositions herein outlined and their cooperation in advocating their adoption by the other powers can be confidently expected. I enclose herewith copy of the instruction which I have sent to Mr. Choate on the subject.

In view of the present favorable conditions, you are instructed to submit the above considerations to His Imperial German Majesty's minister for foreign affairs and to request his early consideration of the subject.

Copy of this instruction is sent to our ambassadors at London and at St. Petersburg for their information.

THEODORE ROOSEVELT: COROLLARY TO THE MONROE DOCTRINE (1905)

Source: *A Compilation of the Messages and Papers of the Presidents 1789–1917,* James D. Richardson, ed., New York, 1920, Vol. XI, pp. 1131–1181.

One of the most effective instruments for peace is the Monroe Doctrine as it has been and is being gradually developed by this nation and accepted by other nations. No other policy could have been as efficient in promoting peace in the Western Hemisphere and in giving to each nation thereon the chance to develop along its own lines. If we had refused to apply the doctrine to changing conditions, it would now be completely outworn, would not meet any of the needs of the present day, and, indeed, would probably by this time have sunk into complete oblivion.

It is useful at home and is meeting with recognition abroad because we have adapted our application of it to meet the growing and changing needs of the Hemisphere. When we announce a policy such as the Monroe Doctrine, we thereby commit ourselves to the consequences of the policy, and those consequences from time to time alter. It is out of the question to claim a right and yet shirk the responsibility for its exercise. Not only we but all American republics who are benefited by the existence of the doctrine must recognize the obligations each nation is under as regards foreign peoples, no less than its duty to insist upon its own rights.

That our rights and interests are deeply concerned in the maintenance of the doctrine is so clear as hardly to need argument. This is especially true in view of the construction of the Panama Canal. As a mere matter of self-defense we must exercise a close watch over the approaches to this canal; and this means that we must be thoroughly alive to our interests in the Caribbean Sea.

There are certain essential points which must never be forgotten as regards the Monroe Doctrine. In the first place, we must as a nation make it evident that we do not intend to treat it in any shape or way as an excuse for aggrandizement on our part at the expense of the republics to the south. We must recognize the fact that in some South American countries there has been much suspicion lest we should interpret the Monroe Doctrine as in some way inimical to their interests, and we must try to convince all the other nations of this continent once and for all that no just and orderly government has anything to fear from us.

There are certain republics to the south of us which have already reached such a point of stability, order, and prosperity that they themselves, though as yet hardly consciously, are among the guarantors of this doctrine. These republics we now meet, not only on a basis of entire equality but in a spirit of frank and respectful friendship, which we hope is mutual. If all of the republics to the south of us will only grow as those to which I allude have already grown, all need for us to be the especial champions of the doctrine will disappear, for no stable and growing American republic wishes to see some great non-American military power acquire territory in its neighborhood. All that this country desires is that the other republics on this continent shall be happy and prosperous; and they cannot be happy and prosperous unless they maintain order within their boundaries and behave with a just regard for their obligations toward outsiders.

It must be understood that under no circumstances will be the United States use the Monroe Doctrine as a cloak for territorial aggression. We desire peace with all the world, but perhaps most of all with the other peoples of the American continent. There are, of course, limits to the wrongs which any self-respecting nation can endure. It is always possible that wrong actions toward this nation or toward citizens of this nation in some state unable to keep order among its own people, unable to secure justice from outsiders, and unwilling to do justice to those outsiders who treat it well, may result in our having to take action to protect our rights; but such action will not be taken with a view to territorial aggression, and it will be taken at all only with extreme reluctance and when it has become evident that every other resource has been exhausted.

Moreover, we must make it evident that we do not intend to permit the Monroe Doctrine to be used by any nation on this continent as a shield to protect it from the consequences of its own misdeeds against foreign nations. If a republic to the south of us commits a tort against a foreign nation, such as an outrage against a citizen of that nation, then the Monroe Doctrine does not force us to interfere to prevent punishment of the tort, save to see that the punishment does not assume the form of territorial occupation in any shape.

The case is more difficult when it refers to a contractual obligation. Our own government has always refused to enforce such contractual obligations on behalf of its citizens by an appeal to arms. It is much to be wished that all foreign governments would take the same view. But they do not; and in consequence we are liable at any time to be brought face to face with disagreeable alternatives. On the one hand, this country would certainly decline to go to war to prevent a foreign government from collecting a just debt; on the other hand, it is very inadvisable to permit any foreign power to take possession, even temporarily, of the custom-houses of an American republic in order to enforce the payment of its obligations; for such temporary occupation might turn into a permanent occupation.

The only escape from these alternatives may at any time be that we must ourselves undertake to bring about some arrangement by which so much as possible of a just obligation shall be paid. It is far better that this country should put through such an arrangement, rather than allow any foreign country to undertake it. To do so insures the defaulting republic from having to pay debt of an improper character under duress, while it also insures honest creditors of the republic from being passed by in the interest of dishonest or grasping creditors. Moreover, for the United States to take such a position offers the only possible way of insuring us against a clash with some foreign power. The position

is, therefore, in the interest of peace as well as in the interest of justice. It is of benefit to our people; it is of benefit to foreign peoples; and most of all it is really of benefit to the people of the country concerned.

This brings me to what should be one of the fundamental objects of the Monroe Doctrine. We must ourselves in good faith try to help upward toward peace and order those of our sister republics which need such help. Just as there has been a gradual growth of the ethical element in the relations of one individual to another, so we are, even though slowly, more and more coming to recognize the duty of bearing one another's burdens, not only as among individuals but also as among nations.

JANE ADDAMS: INDUSTRIAL AMELIORATION AND SOCIAL ETHICS (1902)

Source: *Democracy and Social Ethics*, New York, 1902: "Industrial Amelioration."

The man who disassociates his ambition, however disinterested, from the cooperation of his fellows, always takes [the] risk of ultimate failure. He does not take advantage of the great conserver and guarantee of his own permanent success which associated efforts afford. Genuine experiments toward higher social conditions must have a more democratic faith and practice than those which underlie private venture. Public parks and improvements, intended for the common use, are after all only safe in the hands of the public itself; and associated effort toward social progress, although much more awkward and stumbling than that same effort managed by a capable individual, does yet enlist deeper forces and evoke higher social capacities.

The successful businessman who is also the philanthropist is in more than the usual danger of getting widely separated from his employees. The men already have the American veneration for wealth and successful business capacity, and, added to this, they are dazzled by his good works. The workmen have the same kindly impulses as he, but while they organize their charity into mutual benefit associations and distribute their money in small amounts in relief for the widows and insurance for the injured, the employer may build model towns, erect college buildings, which are tangible and enduring, and thereby display his goodness in concentrated form.

By the very exigencies of business demands, the employer is too often cut off from the social ethics developing in regard to our larger social relationships and from the great moral life springing from our common experiences. This is sure to happen when he is good "to" people rather than "with" them, when he allows himself to decide what is best for them instead of consulting them. He thus misses the rectifying influence of that fellowship which is so big that it leaves no room for sensitiveness or gratitude. Without this fellowship we may never know how great the divergence between

ourselves and others may become, nor how cruel the misunderstandings.

During a recent strike of the employees of a large factory in Ohio, the president of the company expressed himself as bitterly disappointed by the results of his many kindnesses, and evidently considered the employees utterly unappreciative. His state of mind was the result of the fallacy of ministering to social needs from an individual impulse and expecting a socialized return of gratitude and loyalty. If the lunchroom was necessary, it was a necessity in order that the employees might have better food, and, when they had received the better food, the legitimate aim of the lunchroom was met. If baths were desirable, and the fifteen minutes of calisthenic exercise given the women in the middle of each half day brought a needed rest and change to their muscles, then the increased cleanliness and the increased bodily comfort of so many people should of themselves have justified the experiment.

To demand, as a further result, that there should be no strikes in the factory, no revolt against the will of the employer because the employees were filled with loyalty as the result of the kindness, was of course to take the experiment from an individual basis to a social one.

Large mining companies and manufacturing concerns are constantly appealing to their stockholders for funds or for permission to take a percentage of the profits, in order that the money may be used for educational and social schemes designed for the benefit of the employees. The promoters of these schemes use, as an argument and as an appeal, that better relations will be thus established, that strikes will be prevented, and that in the end the money returned to the stockholders will be increased. However praiseworthy this appeal may be in motive, it involves a distinct confusion of issues, and in theory deserves the failure it so often meets with in practice. In the clash which follows a strike, the employees are accused of an ingratitude when there was no legitimate reason to expect gratitude; and useless bitterness, which has really a factitious basis, may be developed on both sides.

Indeed, unless the relation becomes a democratic one, the chances of misunderstanding are increased, when to the relation of employer and employees is added the relation of benefactor to beneficiaries, insofar as there is still another opportunity for acting upon the individual code of ethics.

There is no doubt that these efforts are to be commended, not only from the standpoint of their social value but because they have a marked industrial significance. Failing, as they do, however, to touch the question of wages and hours, which are almost invariably the points of trades union effort, the employers confuse the mind of the public when they urge the amelioration of conditions and the kindly relation existing between them and their men as a reason for the discontinuance of strikes and other trades union tactics. The men have individually accepted the kindness of the employers as it was individually offered, but quite as the latter urges his inability to increase wages unless he has the cooperation of his competitors, so the men state that they are bound to the trades union struggle for an increase in wages because it can only be undertaken by combinations of labor.

Even the much more democratic effort to divide a proportion of the profits at the end of the year among the employees, upon the basis of their wages and efficiency, is also exposed to a weakness, from the fact that the employing side has the power of determining to whom the benefit shall accrue.

Both individual acts of self-defense on the part of the wage earner and individual acts of benevolence on the part of the employer are most useful as they establish standards to which the average worker and employer may in time be legally compelled to conform. Progress must always come through the individual who varies from the type and has sufficient energy to express this variation. He first holds a higher conception than that held by the mass of his fellows of what is righteous under given conditions, and expresses this conviction in conduct, in many instances formulating a certain scruple which the others share but have not yet defined even to themselves.

Progress, however, is not secure until the mass has conformed to this new righteousness. This is equally true in regard to any advance made in the standard of living on the part of the trades unionists or in the improved conditions of industry on the part of reforming employers.

The mistake lies, not in overpraising the advance thus inaugurated by individual initiative but in regarding the achievement as complete in a social sense when it is still in the realm of individual action.

No sane manufacturer regards his factory as the center of the industrial system. He knows very well that the cost of material, wages, and selling prices are determined by industrial conditions completely beyond his control. Yet the same man may quite calmly regard himself and his own private principles as merely self-regarding and expect results from casual philanthropy which can only be accomplished through those common rules of life and labor established by the community for the common good.

Outside of and surrounding these smaller and most significant efforts are the larger and irresistible movements operating toward combination. This movement must tend to decide upon social matters from the social standpoint. Until then it is difficult to keep our minds free from a confusion of issues. Such a confusion occurs when the gift of a large sum to the community for a public and philanthropic purpose throws a certain glamor over all the earlier acts of a man and makes it difficult for the community to see possible wrongs committed against it in the accumulation of wealth so beneficently used. It is possible also that the resolve to be thus generous unconsciously influences the man himself in his methods of accumulation. He keeps to a certain individual rectitude, meaning to make an individual restitution by the old paths of generosity and kindness, whereas if he had in view social restitution on the newer lines of justice and opportunity, he would throughout his course doubtless be watchful of his industrial relationships and his social virtues.

The danger of professionally attaining to the power of the righteous man, of yielding to the ambition "for doing good" on a large scale, compared to which the ambition for politics, learning, or wealth are vulgar and commonplace, ramifies through our modern life; and those most easily beset by this temptation are precisely the men best situated to experiment on the larger social lines, because they so easily dramatize their acts and lead public opinion. Very often, too, they have in their hands the preservation and advancement of large vested interests, and often see clearly and truly that they are better able to administer the affairs of the community than the community itself; sometimes they see that if they do not administer them sharply and quickly, as only an individual can, certain interests of theirs dependent upon the community will go to ruin.

The model employer first considered provided a large sum in his will with which to build and equip a polytechnic school, which will doubtless be of great public value. This again shows the advantage of individual management, in the spending as well as in the accumulating of wealth, but this school will attain its highest good, insofar as it incites the ambition to provide other schools from public funds. The town of Zurich possesses a magnificent polytechnic institute, secured by the vote of the entire people and supported from public taxes. Every man who voted for it is interested that his child should enjoy its benefits, and, of course, the voluntary attendance must be larger than in a school accepted as a gift to the community.

In the educational efforts of model employers, as in other attempts toward social amelioration, one man with the best of intentions is trying to do what the entire body of employees should have undertaken to do for themselves. The result of his efforts will only attain its highest value as it serves as an incentive to procure other results by the community as well as for the community.

There are doubtless many things which the public would never demand unless they were first supplied by individual initiative, both because the public lacks the imagination and also the power of formulating their wants. Thus philanthropic effort supplies kindergartens, until they become so established in the popular affections that they are incorporated in the public school system. Churches and missions establish reading rooms, until at last the public library system dots the city with branch reading rooms and libraries. For this willingness to take risks for the sake of an ideal, for those experiments which must be undertaken with vigor and boldness in order to secure didactic value in failure as well as in success, society must depend upon the individual possessed with money, and

also distinguished by earnest and unselfish purpose.

Such experiments enable the nation to use the referendum method in its public affairs. Each social experiment is thus tested by a few people, given wide publicity that it may be observed and discussed by the bulk of the citizens before the public prudently makes up its mind whether or not it is wise to incorporate it into the functions of government. If the decision is in its favor and it is so incorporated, it can then be carried on with confidence and enthusiasm.

But experience has shown that we can only depend upon successful men for a certain type of experiment in the line of industrial amelioration and social advancement. The list of those who found churches, educational institutions, libraries, and art galleries is very long, as is again the list of those contributing to model dwellings, recreation halls, and athletic fields. At the present moment factory employers are doing much to promote "industrial betterment" in the way of sanitary surroundings, opportunities for bathing, lunchrooms provided with cheap and wholesome food, clubrooms, and guild halls.

But there is a line of social experiment involving social righteousness in its most advanced form, in which the number of employers and the "favored class" are so few that it is plain society cannot count upon them for continuous and valuable help. This lack is in the line of factory legislation and that sort of social advance implied in shorter hours and the regulation of wages; in short, all that organization and activity that is involved in such a maintenance and increase of wages as would prevent the lowering of the standard of life.

A large body of people feel keenly that the present industrial system is in a state of profound disorder and that there is no guarantee that the pursuit of individual ethics will ever right it. They claim that relief can only come through deliberate corporate effort inspired by social ideas and guided by the study of economic laws, and that the present industrial system thwarts our ethical demands, not only for social righteousness but for social order. Because they believe that each advance in ethics must be made fast by a corresponding advance in politics and legal enactment, they insist upon the right of state regulation and control. While many people representing all classes in a community would assent to this as to a general proposition, and would even admit it as a certain moral obligation, legislative enactments designed to control industrial conditions have largely been secured through the efforts of a few citizens, mostly those who constantly see the harsh conditions of labor and who are incited to activity by their sympathies as well as their convictions.

This may be illustrated by the series of legal enactments regulating the occupations in which children may be allowed to work, also the laws in regard to the hours of labor permitted in those occupations, and the minimum age below which children may not be employed. The first child labor laws were enacted in England through the efforts of those members of Parliament whose hearts were wrung by the condition of the little parish apprentices bound out to the early textile manufacturers of the North; and through the long years required to build up the code of child labor legislation which England now possesses, knowledge of the conditions has always preceded effective legislation.

The efforts of that small number in every community who believe in legislative control have always been reenforced by the efforts of trades unionists rather than by the efforts of employers. Partly because the employment of workingmen in the factories brings them in contact with the children who tend to lower wages and demoralize their trades, and partly because workingmen have no money nor time to spend in alleviating philanthropy, and must perforce seize upon agitation and legal enactment as the only channel of redress which is open to them.

We may illustrate by imagining a row of people seated in a moving streetcar, into which darts a boy of eight, calling out the details of the last murder in the hope of selling an evening newspaper. A comfortable looking man buys a paper from him with no sense of moral shock; he may even be a trifle complacent that he has helped along the little fellow, who is making his way in the world. The philanthropic lady sitting next to him may perhaps reflect that it is a pity that such a bright boy is not in school. She may make up her mind in a moment of compunction to redouble her efforts for various newsboys' schools and homes that this poor child may have better teaching and, perhaps, a chance at manual training. She probably is convinced that he alone, by his unaided efforts, is supporting a widowed mother, and her heart is moved to do all she can for him.

Next to her sits a workingman trained in trades union methods. He knows that the boy's natural development is arrested and that the abnormal activity of his body and mind uses up the force which should go into growth; moreover, that this premature use of his powers has but a momentary and specious value. He is forced to these conclusions because he has seen many a man, entering the factory at eighteen and twenty, so worn out by premature work that he was "laid on the shelf" within ten or fifteen years. He knows very well that he can do nothing in the way of ameliorating the lot of this particular boy; that his only possible chance is to agitate for proper child labor laws; to regulate, and if possible prohibit, street vending by children in order that the child of the poorest may have his schooltime secured to him, and may have at least his short chance for growth.

These three people, sitting in the streetcar, are all honest and upright, and recognize a certain duty toward the forlorn children of the community. The self-made man is encouraging one boy's own efforts; the philanthropic lady is helping on a few boys; the workingman alone is obliged to include all the boys of his class. Workingmen, because of their feebleness in all but numbers, have been forced to appeal to the state in order to secure protection for themselves and for their children. They cannot all rise out of their class, as the occasionally successful man has done; some of them must be left to do the work in the factories and mines, and they have no money to spend in philanthropy.

Both public agitation and a social appeal to the conscience of the community is necessary in order to secure help from the state, and, curiously enough, child labor laws once enacted and enforced are a matter of great pride, and even come to be regarded as a register of the community's humanity and enlightenment. If the method of public agitation could find quiet and orderly expression in legislative enactment, and if labor measures could be submitted to the examination and judgment of the whole without a sense of division or of warfare, we should have the ideal development of the democratic state.

But we judge labor organizations as we do other living institutions, not by their declaration of principles, which we seldom read, but by their blundering efforts to apply their principles to actual conditions, and by the oft-time failure of their representatives, when the individual finds himself too weak to become the organ of corporate action.

The very blunders and lack of organization too often characterizing a union, in marked contrast to the orderly management of a factory, often confuse us as to the real issues involved, and we find it hard to trust uncouth and unruly manifestations of social effort. The situation is made even more complicated by the fact that those who are formulating a code of associated action so often break through the established code of law and order.

As society has a right to demand of the reforming individual that he be sternly held to his personal and domestic claims, so it has a right to insist that labor organizations shall keep to the hardly won standards of public law and order; and the community performs but its plain duty when it registers its protest every time law and order are subverted, even in the interest of the so-called social effort. Yet in moments of industrial stress and strain the community is confronted by a moral perplexity which may arise from the mere fact that the good of yesterday is opposed to the good of today, and that which may appear as a choice between virtue and vice is really but a choice between virtue and virtue. In the disorder and confusion sometimes incident to growth and progress, the community may be unable to see anything but the unlovely struggle itself....

At times of social disturbance the law-abiding citizen is naturally so anxious for peace and order, his sympathies are so justly and inevitably on the side making for the restoration of law, that it is difficult for him to see the situation fairly. He becomes insensible to the unselfish impulse which may prompt a sympathetic strike in behalf of the workers in a non-union shop because he allows his mind to dwell exclusively on the disorder which has become associated with the strike. He is completely sidetracked by the ugly phases of a great moral movement. It is always a temptation to assume that the side which has respectability, authority, and superior intelligence has therefore righteousness as well, especially when the same side presents concrete results of individual effort as over against the less tangible results of associated effort.

It is as yet most difficult for us to free ourselves from the individualistic point of view sufficiently to group events in their social relations and to judge fairly those who are endeavoring to produce a social result through all the difficulties of associated action. The philanthropist still finds his path much easier than do those who are attempting a social morality. In the first place, the public, anxious to praise what it recognizes as an undoubted moral effort often attended with real personal sacrifice, joyfully seizes upon this manifestation and overpraises it, recognizing the philanthropist as an old friend in the paths of righteousness, whereas the others are strangers and possibly to be distrusted as aliens.

It is easy to confuse the response to an abnormal number of individual claims with the response to the social claim. An exaggerated personal morality is often mistaken for a social morality, and until it attempts to minister to a social situation its total inadequacy is not discovered. To attempt to attain a social morality without a basis of democratic experience results in the loss of the only possible corrective and guide, and ends in an exaggerated individual morality but not in social morality at all. We see this from time to time in the careworn and overworked philanthropist, who has taxed his individual will beyond the normal limits and has lost his clue to the situation among a bewildering number of cases.

A man who takes the betterment of humanity for his aim and end must also take the daily experiences of humanity for the constant correction of his process. He must not only test and guide his achievement by human experience but he must succeed or fail in proportion as he has incorporated that experience with his own. Otherwise, his own achievements become his stumbling block, and he comes to believe in his own goodness as something outside of himself. He makes an exception of himself and thinks that he is different from the rank and file of his fellows. He forgets that it is necessary to know of the lives of our contemporaries, not only in order to believe in their integrity, which is after all but the first beginnings of social morality, but in order to attain to any mental or moral integrity for ourselves or any such hope for society.

AMOS P. WILDER: "GOVERNOR LA FOLLETTE AND WHAT HE STANDS FOR" (1902)

Source: *Outlook*, March 8, 1902.

In Wisconsin the political issues are two: the direct vote in making nominations, thus bringing political control back to the people; and the forcing of corporations to bear their share of taxation. A most trustworthy state Tax Commission reported a year ago that tax reform should begin by adding over $1,200,000 every two years to the amounts already paid by the railroads. The last legislature refused to enact the increase. Can a legislature be secured that will do its duty?

Wisconsin people are not more Populistic than other well-fed, genial Americans who tolerate bathtubs in their homes and accept Carnegie libraries. But many of them believe that the unfolding life of the nation reveals new dangers to guard against; and it has not escaped attention that the nominating of candidates has become a confused and remote process, and that too often the men of power in political councils are the controlling forces in quasi-public corporations which desire favorable legislation. Wealth seeks to fortify itself with all the concomitants of ability, power, and secrecy. Personality is at work, both coercive and persuasive. There is intrigue, indecision, and the play of vice on weakness. The fighters are taking their posts. There is the cry of challenge and defiance.

Meanwhile, the electorate, a body of over 450,000 voters, mostly agriculturists—men of Wisconsin, sons of New England, Germans, Norwegians, and representatives of many other lands—look confusedly on, waiting for the contest to begin. As in all war, the people pay the bills, carry the burdens, and suffer the distress, but they may also profit by a victory. Governor La Follette, whose reelection is the issue, insists that their interests lie his way. The election occurs in November next. The state Republican convention, which will name the candidate for governor, meets during the summer. The immediate object of the present contest is to secure a majority of the delegates from the seventy counties to this convention and control it.

Governor La Follette is popularly regarded as the standard bearer of reform. He is now serving his first term, and the effort of his opponents is to crush him before he gets any further. Whether one regards this interesting figure as a young David defying the giant of capital and the established order, or brands him as a clever opportunist and a silver-tongued demagogue, will decide one's enrollment, in Wisconsin parlance, as a "half-breed" or a "stalwart." Most of the newspapers are working for his defeat, and not a few of them have shifted their attitude under suspicious circumstances. The adroit opposition has just now complicated the situation and confounded the voters by proposing as their candidate against Governor La Follette a man not only of recognized purity and wisdom but of great determination and aggressive integrity.

Let us consider some of the factors that veil this struggle to get power back to the hands of the people. Governor La

Follette is forty-seven years old, but all think of him as young. His family stock was of "the people" and of the soil—a coveted prestige in this Northwest, where farmers control things. La Follette made a reputation in his university days as an orator, but he was too busy earning his living to do much with books. He won the intercollegiate contest when a number of states sent their best college speakers to Iowa City. His oration, an original study of Iago, is still quoted in the district schools. Like many men of the public type, La Follette is strongly endowed with the dramatic instinct. He is short in stature but shapely, with a striking face and head, smooth-shaven, and with abundant dark hair piled up on a high forehead.

He was taken up by the voters when scarcely out of the law school and was made district attorney; then he served six years in Congress—from 1885 to 1891. He was on William McKinley's committee that framed the McKinley tariff, and the Ohio leader thought much of the young man from Wisconsin. For some years, after the Democratic tidal wave of 1890 retired him from Congress, Mr. La Follette practised law. He achieved distinction in jury work, but the attractions of political life were too strong for him, and in 1896 he offered himself to the Republicans for the nomination as governor.

They declined to accept him. In 1898 he tried it again. By this time he had formulated his reforms. He was again defeated, but his platform compelled acceptance. The oldline Republicans, who had long before instinctively felt that he was no longer their kind, were now worried, and their fears were justified. La Follette got out among "the people," spoke to them and with them, and soon had them enthusiastically behind him. In 1900 he received the nomination unanimously, not because the machine wanted him but because it had to take him. He polled the full vote and, with McKinley, secured over a 100,000 Republican majority.

The political methods of any man who can overthrow so well-approved a machine as that which has been built up in Wisconsin merit consideration. He did it by building up an even better machine.

In a campaign, Governor La Follette is a tireless worker, attracting to himself, by his magnetic personality, young men, especially university graduates and young lawyers; and his own law office is a hive of industry. By personal letters and printed documents he reaches great numbers of men of local influence in all the seventy counties of the state. Mrs. La Follette was a classmate of her husband, an unusual woman, interested in advance movements, and an enthusiastic coworker with him in his public ambition. The governor is a man of blameless personal life, of a sanguine disposition, strong in his likes and dislikes, and styled by his enemies "a dictator" and "vindictive."

He works best with lieutenants who obey without question. It was said of Horatio Seymour that he worked well in any sort of harness. Governor La Follette

is not of this class of men. His temperament is on the order of Mr. Bryan's; he is eager to be the people's champion; his mind is aglow with visions of great enactments for the public welfare. Commingled with this is great personal ambition. Men of this stamp wish to be at the head of the procession, not merely in it; and the enactments must bear their name. Only superficial estimators of character and usefulness, however, are dismayed by these outcroppings of human nature. Indeed, one must be prepared to tolerate even cruder forms of human nature to comprehend the potential usefulness of men like La Follette and those who grapple with the modern lions that guard the portals where privilege is entrenched.

With Governor La Follette's stronghold on the common people goes great power as a political organizer and much political adroitness, to which his enemies give a stronger name. This reformer, unlike some others, is not only bold but very shrewd; the children of darkness must look to themselves when pitted against La Follette. His third and successful convention, the one of last summer, is an illustration. After a stormy anti-convention fight, in which La Follette stirred the state as an anti-corporation champion, the remarkable spectacle of a unanimous convention and nomination ensued, and among the workers in the campaign which gave La Follette an unprecedented majority none was more diligent than the railroads. The sudden falling in line of the managers of the railroads and other corporations for

La Follette was something of a mystery; some of the other candidates believed that he had come to an understanding with the influential political managers. The friends of the governor assert what I believe to be true, that he had his enemies "on the run"; by brilliant campaign organization in the pivotal counties he routed them. It was then for them a case of "bandwagon."

Governor La Follette does things that weary the patience of the most loyal adherent. So dominant is his personality that many independent men are alienated. He has put men up for office whose characters were objectionable and whose qualifications were pitiful. But through his appointments and policies runs a vein of political purpose. The governor takes all that apply, saints and sinners alike, and there are fishes for the hungry. In his second and successful campaign to secure the governorship, he made a mercilessly persistent attack on Governor Scofield, an excellent executive—one of the honorable order of sawmill owners who have long served Wisconsin in public station. It was hard to see any reason why Scofield should be thrown out and La Follette put in, except that the latter wanted to "lead the people."

And yet, notwithstanding these facts, the man is strong and is really a leader of the people. Why? Because he is honest and fearless and stands for something. Given these qualities and it is amazing how much the electorate will overlook. It suddenly flashes into the minds of the electorate how inspiring is a man with a clear-cut mission, and how rare is the combination of honesty and courage in American public life— so rare when it comes to assailing the castle of privilege and custom that even wisdom is not an indispensable handmaid. It requires some such view of the exigencies of latterday politics to understand Robert La Follette's position in Wisconsin and why the people cling to him when the ranks of conventionality, wealth, and distinction have pretty generally branded him as a disturber and even a charlatan.

The legislative session of 1900 was stormy almost from the beginning. La Follette sought to crowd through a primary election bill. It was a drastic measure. The party platform promised such a law. It was the one issue about which the entire session of five months raged. The governor was able to pass it in the Assembly by a close vote; but the senators developed opposition to his measure and to him personally, and the feeling ran very high, culminating at the close in a veto of a partial primary measure which the opposition offered him, as he believed, to embarrass him. This veto message scored his enemies in the most scorching language. He charged the opponents of the primary election bill with getting members drunk and tempting them with vice to secure their votes. The Outlook said at the time that it was the most vigorous public utterance made in this country for a generation. The opposition senators put on record their assertion that it was insulting.

One of the first steps taken to crush the governor was the purchase of one of the greatest of the Milwaukee dailies, with a circulation throughout the state, its editorial policy being reversed in one day. Soon after the legislature adjourned, the "stalwart" Republican League was formed. On the face of it this call to a reorganization of the party seemed unanswerable; it was signed by eighteen of the thirty-one Republican senators and by eighty-one of the Republican assemblymen, and there were many good men among them. A palatial suite of rooms was engaged in Milwaukee, and for months it has been the headquarters of an anti-La Follette campaign, which for lavish expenditure, bitterness, and persistent effort has rarely been equaled.

State Senator John M. Whitehead (Yale, 1877) has been called upon by the opposition to dispute the nomination with Governor La Follette and has formally accepted the proposition that he should contest the nomination. Mr. Whitehead is a lawyer and a man of the highest character and of unusual force and judgment. He is president of the state Young Men's Christian Association; a big, determined, honest fellow, with no humor, but on intimate terms with grim duty as he sees it. Normally, his would be a candidacy for all well-disposed citizens to get behind. The movement, however, which is urging this candidacy, while statewide in its personnel, will be under "stalwart" auspices; and those who distrust the movement will be tempted to say that Whitehead's candidacy is analogous to Shepard's support and nomination by Tammany Hall.

La Follette is the present hope of "primary elections" in Wisconsin. This interests him more than anything else. Some of his opponents say that it is his scheme to build up a state machine. Many regard the principle as an absurdity; these are the uninformed. The ringsters, of course, are instinctively opposed to allowing the voters to have any more to do with the nominations than necessary. This great reform, which is engaging the attention of thoughtful men in many states, finds its champion in Wisconsin in Governor La Follette. He is eager to further it—not necessarily in the sweeping form in which it was presented to the last legislature but in some fairly advanced way, in order to put the principle on its feet in Wisconsin.

As to the state Tax Commission, all Republicans claim to be its friends; and it is necessary to look beneath the surface. Those interests which object to bigger taxes are in the "stalwart" camp; they presumably pay freely toward the bills of the organization and seek to accomplish their ends largely through its power and machinery. Cooperating with them for the defeat of La Follette are many disinterested citizens who favor aggressive work by the Commission. These are the men who cannot stand for what they call "La Folletteism." They shrink from the governor's methods or question his sincerity. Not a few of the representative men of Wisconsin, including a majority of those who figure in high places at Washington, are of this number. Senator Whitehead, the selected candidate against La

Follette, is known as the "Father of the Tax Commission." I think it can fairly be said that the La Follette forces in the last legislature averaged better as legislators for the people than the stalwarts. It is on this belief that many will support La Follette.

There are times when measures are above men. There are campaigns in which the issue is not the success or overthrow of men but approval or discrediting of a principle. The principle involved in Wisconsin is popular control. The opposition has sneered at primary elections and insists that it was a La Follette scheme to entrench himself, with the aid of typewriters, by sending his literature into the smallest hamlet; but the proposal that citizens get together and indicate on secret ballot whom they would have for mayor and whom they would send to the legislature and to Congress will not down. It commends itself over the present plan of voting for a lot of delegates, whom the citizen does not know, who are to go to some place, perhaps in another county, and vote for some person not specified. La Follette stands for the direct vote.

His opponents say that he has not stood squarely always for vigorous tax reform, but the fact remains that there are now no tax dodgers in his train. For La Follette's political excesses much excuse can be found in the terrific power and wealth pitted against him. He was the one man able to overturn the oligarchy whose rule for years bred recurring restlessness. He may be dictatorial—many leaders are—but it is impossible to conceive him

as anyone's tool. The lobby still lives, but it has no hold in the executive chamber.

If he is renominated and reelected, it will be because the voters strike an average, because his merits outweigh his faults, and because the obvious untrustworthiness of the "Republican League" outweighs in the balance the confessed virtue of many of its upholders. The stalwart League will be dominated, not by the many excellent citizens on its outskirts but by the handful of adroit, tireless professionals who find La Follette an obstacle in the way of corporate control of the political machinery of the state.

MANIFESTO OF THE INDUSTRIAL WORKERS OF THE WORLD (1905)

Source: *Proceedings of the First Convention of the Industrial Workers of the World*, New York, n.d., pp. 3–6.

Social relations and groupings only reflect mechanical and industrial conditions. The great facts of present industry are the displacement of human skill by machines and the increase of capitalist power through concentration in the possession of the tools with which wealth is produced and distributed.

Because of these facts, trade divisions among laborers and competition among capitalists are alike disappearing. Class divisions grow ever more fixed and class antagonisms more sharp. Trade lines have been swallowed up in a common servitude of all workers to the machines which they tend. New machines, ever replacing less productive ones, wipe out whole trades and plunge new bodies of workers into the ever growing army of tradeless, hopeless unemployed. As human beings and human skill are displaced by mechanical progress, the capitalists need use the workers only during that brief period when muscles and nerves respond most intensely. The moment the laborer no longer yields the maximum of profits, he is thrown upon the scrap pile, to starve alongside the discarded machine. A dead line has been drawn, and an age limit established, to cross which, in this world of monopolized opportunities, means condemnation to industrial death.

The worker, wholly separated from the land and the tools, with his skill of craftsmanship rendered useless, is sunk in the uniform mass of wage slaves. He sees his power of resistance broken by craft divisions, perpetuated from outgrown industrial stages. His wages constantly grow less as his hours grow longer and monopolized prices grow higher. Shifted hither and thither by the demands of profit-takers, the laborer's home no longer exists. In this helpless condition he is forced to accept whatever humiliating conditions his master may impose. He is submitted to a physical and intellectual examination more searching than was the chattel slave when sold from the auction block.

Laborers are no longer classified by differences in trade skill, but the employer assigns them according to the machines to which they are attached.

These divisions, far from representing differences in skill or interests among the laborers, are imposed by the employers that workers may be pitted against one another and spurred to greater exertion in the shop, and that all resistance to capitalist tyranny may be weakened by artificial distinctions.

While encouraging these outgrown divisions among the workers, the capitalists carefully adjust themselves to the new conditions. They wipe out all differences among themselves and present a united front in their war upon labor. Through employers' associations, they seek to crush, with brutal force, by the injunctions of the judiciary and the use of military power, all efforts at resistance. Or when the other policy seems more profitable, they conceal their daggers beneath the Civic Federation and hoodwink and betray those whom they would rule and exploit. Both methods depend for success upon the blindness and internal dissensions of the working class. The employers' line of battle and methods of warfare correspond to the solidarity of the mechanical and industrial concentration, while laborers still form their fighting organizations on lines of long-gone trade divisions.

The battles of the past emphasize this lesson. The textile workers of Lowell, Philadelphia, and Fall River; the butchers of Chicago, weakened by the disintegrating effects of trade divisions; the machinists on the Santa Fe, unsupported by their fellow workers subject to the same masters; the long-struggling miners of Colorado, hampered by lack of unity and solidarity upon the industrial battlefield, all bear witness to the helplessness and impotency of labor as at present organized.

This worn-out and corrupt system offers no promise of improvement and adaptation. There is no silver lining to the clouds of darkness and despair settling down upon the world of labor. This system offers only a perpetual struggle for slight relief within wage slavery. It is blind to the possibility of establishing an industrial democracy wherein there shall be no wage slavery, but where the workers will own the tools which they operate and the product of which they alone will enjoy.

It shatters the ranks of the workers into fragments, rendering them helpless and impotent on the industrial battlefield.

Separation of craft from craft renders industrial and financial solidarity impossible. Union men scab upon union men; hatred of worker for worker is engendered, and the workers are delivered helpless and disintegrated into the hands of the capitalists. Craft jealousy leads to the attempt to create trade monopolies.

Prohibitive initiation fees are established that force men to become scabs against their will. Men whom manliness or circumstances have driven from one trade are thereby fined when they seek to transfer membership to the union of a new craft.

Craft divisions foster political ignorance among the workers, thus dividing their class at the ballot box as well as in the shop, mine, and factory.

Craft unions may be and have been used to assist employers in the establishment of monopolies and the raising of prices. One set of workers are thus used to make harder the conditions of life of another body of laborers.

Craft divisions hinder the growth of class consciousness of the workers, foster the idea of harmony of interests between employing exploiter and employed slave. They permit the association of the misleaders of the workers with the capitalists in the civic federations, where plans are made for the perpetuation of capitalism and the permanent enslavement of the workers through the wage system.

Previous efforts for the betterment of the working class have proven abortive because limited in scope and disconnected in action.

Universal economic evils afflicting the working class can be eradicated only by a universal working-class movement. Such a movement of the working class is impossible while separate craft and wage agreements are made favoring the employer against other crafts in the same industry and while energies are wasted in fruitless jurisdiction struggles which serve only to further the personal aggrandizement of union officials.

A movement to fulfill these conditions must consist of one great industrial union embracing all industries, providing for craft autonomy locally, industrial autonomy internationally, and working-class unity generally. It must be founded on the class struggle, and its general administration must be conducted in harmony with the recognition of the irrepressible conflict between the capitalist class and the working class. It should be established as the economic organization of the working class, without affiliation with any political party.

All power should rest in a collective membership.

Local, national, and general administration, including union labels, buttons, badges, transfer cards, initiation fees, and per capita tax should be uniform throughout.

All members must hold membership in the local, national, or international union covering the industry in which they are employed, but transfers of membership between unions, local, national, or international, should be universal.

Workingmen bringing union cards from industrial unions in foreign countries should be freely admitted into the organization.

The general administration should issue a publication representing the entire union and its principles which should reach all members in every industry at regular intervals.

A central defense fund, to which all members contribute equally, should be established and maintained.

All workers, therefore, who agree with the principles herein set forth, will meet in convention at Chicago the 27th day of June, 1905, for the purpose of forming an economic organization of the working class along the lines marked out in this manifesto.

Representation in the convention shall be based upon the number of workers whom the delegate represents. No delegate, however, shall be given representation in the convention on the numerical basis of an organization unless he has credentials bearing the seal of his union, local, national or international, and the signatures of the officers thereof, authorizing him to install his union as a working part of the proposed economic organization in the industrial department in which it logically belongs in the general plan of organization. Lacking this authority, the delegate shall represent himself as an individual.

WILLIAM HOWARD TAFT: DEFENSE OF A HIGH TARIFF (1909)

Source: 61 Congress, 2 Session, Senate Document No. 164.

As long ago as August 1906, in the congressional campaign in Maine, I ventured to announce that I was a tariff revisionist and thought that the time had come for a readjustment of the schedules. I pointed out that it had been ten years prior to that time that the Dingley Bill had been passed; that great changes had taken place in the conditions surrounding the productions of the farm, the factory, and the mine, and that under the theory of protection in that time the rates imposed in the Dingley Bill in many instances might have become excessive; that is, might have been greater than the difference between the cost of production abroad and the cost of production at home, with a sufficient allowance for a reasonable rate of profit to the American producer.

I said that the party was divided on the issue, but that in my judgment the opinion of the party was crystallizing and would probably result in the near future in an effort to make such revision. I pointed out the difficulty that there always was in a revision of the tariff, due to the threatened disturbance of industries to be affected and the suspension of business, in a way which made it unwise to have too many revisions.

In the summer of 1907 my position on the tariff was challenged, and I then entered into a somewhat fuller discussion of the matter. It was contended by the so-called standpatters that rates beyond the necessary measure of protection were not objectionable because behind the tariff wall competition always reduced the prices and thus saved the consumer. But I pointed out in that speech what seems to me as true today as it then was, that the danger of excessive rates was in the temptation they created to form monopolies in the protected articles, and thus to take advantage of the excessive rates by increasing the prices, and therefore, and in order to avoid such a danger, it was wise at regular intervals to examine the question of what the effect of the rates had been upon the industries in this country, and whether the conditions with respect to the cost of production here had

so changed as to warrant a reduction in the tariff, and to make a lower rate truly protective of the industry.

It will be observed that the object of the revision under such a statement was not to destroy protected industries in this country but it was to continue to protect them where lower rates offered a sufficient protection to prevent injury by foreign competition. That was the object of the revision as advocated by me, and it was certainly the object of the revision as promised in the Republican platform.

I want to make as clear as I can this proposition, because, in order to determine whether a bill is a compliance with the terms of that platform, it must be understood what the platform means. A free trader is opposed to any protective rate because he thinks that our manufacturers, our farmers, and our miners ought to withstand the competition of foreign manufacturers and miners and farmers, or else go out of business and find something else more profitable to do. Now, certainly the promises of the platform did not contemplate the downward revision of the tariff rates to such a point that any industry theretofore protected should be injured. Hence, those who contend that the promise of the platform was to reduce prices by letting in foreign competition are contending for a free trade and not for anything that they had the right to infer from the Republican platform.

The Ways and Means Committee of the House, with Mr. Payne at its head, spent a full year in an investigation, assembling evidence in reference to the rates under the tariff, and devoted an immense amount of work in the study of the question where the tariff rates could be reduced and where they ought to be raised with a view to maintaining a reasonably protective rate, under the principles of the platform, for every industry that deserved protection. They found that the determination of the question, what was the actual cost of production and whether an industry in this country could live under a certain rate and withstand threatened competition from abroad, was most difficult. The manufacturers were prone to exaggerate the injury which a reduction in the duty would give and to magnify the amount of duty that was needed; while the importers, on the other hand, who were interested in developing the importation from foreign shores, were quite likely to be equally biased on the other side.

Mr. Payne reported a bill—the Payne Tariff Bill—which went to the Senate and was amended in the Senate by increasing the duty on some things and decreasing it on others. The difference between the House bill and the Senate bill was very much less than the newspapers represented. It turns out upon examination that the reductions in the Senate were about equal to those in the House, though they differed in character.

Now, there is nothing quite so difficult as the discussion of a tariff bill, for the reason that it covers so many different items, and the meaning of the terms and the percentages are very hard to understand. The passage of a new bill, especially where a change in the method of assessing the duties has been followed, presents an opportunity for various modes and calculations of the percentages of increases and decreases that are most misleading and really throw no light at all upon the changes made.

One way of stating what was done is to say what the facts show—that under the Dingley law there were 2,024 items. This included dutiable items only. The Payne law leaves 1,150 of these items unchanged. There are decreases in 654 of the items and increases in 220 of the items. Now, of course, that does not give a full picture, but it does show the proportion of decreases to have been three times those of the increases....

Now, the promise of the Republican platform was not to revise everything downward, and in the speeches which have been taken as interpreting that platform which I made in the campaign, I did not promise that everything should go downward. What I promised was that there should be many decreases, and that in some few things increases would be found to be necessary; but that on the whole I conceived that the change of conditions would make the revision necessarily downward—and that, I contend, under the showing which I have made, has been the result of the Payne Bill. I did not agree, nor did the Republican Party agree, that we would reduce rates to such a point as to reduce prices by the introduction of foreign competition. That is what the free traders desire. That is what the revenue tariff reformers desire; but that is not what the Republican platform promised, and it is not what the Republican Party wished to bring about.

To repeat the statement with which I opened this speech, the proposition of the Republican Party was to reduce rates so as to maintain a difference between the cost of production abroad and the cost of production here, insuring a reasonable profit to the manufacturer on all articles produced in this country; and the proposition to reduce rates and prevent their being excessive was to avoid the opportunity for monopoly and the suppression of competition, so that the excessive rates could be taken advantage of to force prices up.

Now, it is said that there was not a reduction in a number of the schedules where there should have been. It is said that there was no reduction in the cotton schedule. There was not. The House and the Senate took evidence and found from cotton manufacturers and from other sources that the rates upon the lower class of cottons were such as to enable them to make a decent profit—but only a decent profit—and they were contented with it; but that the rates on the higher grades of cotton cloth, by reason of court decisions, had been reduced so that they were considerably below those of the cheaper grades of cotton cloth, and that by undervaluations and otherwise the whole cotton schedule had been made unjust and the various items were disproportionate in respect to the varying cloths.

Hence, in the Senate, a new system was introduced attempting to make the duties more specific rather than ad valorem in order to prevent by judicial decision or otherwise a disproportionate and unequal operation of the schedule. Under this schedule it was contended that there had been a general rise of all the duties on cotton. This was vigorously denied by the experts of the Treasury Department. At last, the Senate, in conference, consented to a reduction amounting to about 10 percent on all the lower grades of cotton, and this reduced the lower grades of cotton substantially to the same rates as before and increased the higher grades to what they ought to be under the Dingley law and what they were intended to be.

Now, I am not going into the question of evidence as to whether the cotton duties were too high and whether the difference between the cost of production abroad and at home, allowing for a reasonable profit to the manufacturer here, is less than the duties which are imposed under the Payne Bill. It was a question of evidence which Congress passed upon, after they heard the statements of cotton manufacturers and such other evidence as they could avail themselves of. I agree that the method of taking evidence and the determination was made in a general way and that there ought to be other methods of obtaining evidence and reaching a conclusion more satisfactory....

On the whole, however, I am bound to say that I think the Payne Tariff Bill is the best tariff bill that the Republican

Party ever passed; that in it the party has conceded the necessity for following the changed conditions and reducing tariff rates accordingly. This is a substantial achievement in the direction of lower tariffs and downward revision, and it ought to be accepted as such. Critics of the bill utterly ignore the very tremendous cuts that have been made in the iron schedule which heretofore has been subject to criticism in all tariff bills....

The high cost of living, of which 50 percent is consumed in food, 25 percent in clothing, and 25 percent in rent and fuel, has not been produced by the tariff, because the tariff has remained the same while the increases have gone on. It is due to the change of conditions the world over. Living has increased everywhere in cost—in countries where there is free trade and in countries where there is protection—and that increase has been chiefly seen in the cost of food products. In other words, we have had to pay more for the products of the farmer—for meat, for grain, for everything that enters into food. Now, certainly no one will contend that protection has increased the cost of food in this country, when the fact is that we have been the greatest exporters of food products in the world. It is only that the demand has increased beyond the supply, that farmlands have not been opened as rapidly as the population, and the demand has increased.

I am not saying that the tariff does not increase prices in clothing and in building and in other items that enter into the necessities of life, but what I wish to emphasize is that the recent increases in the cost of living in this country have not been due to the tariff. We have a much higher standard of living in this country than they have abroad, and this has been made possible by higher income for the workingman, the farmer, and all classes. Higher wages have been made possible by the encouragement of diversified industries, built up and fostered by the tariff.

Now, the revision downward of the tariff that I have favored will not, I hope, destroy the industries of the country. Certainly it is not intended to. All that it is intended to do, and that is what I wish to repeat, is to put the tariff where it will protect industries here from foreign competition but will not enable those who will wish to monopolize to raise prices by taking advantage of excessive rates beyond the normal difference in the cost of production.

If the country desires free trade, and the country desires a revenue tariff and wishes the manufacturers all over the country to go out of business, and to have cheaper prices at the expense of the sacrifice of many of our manufacturing interests, then it ought to say so and ought to put the Democratic Party in power if it thinks that party can be trusted to carry out any affirmative policy in favor of a revenue tariff. Certainly in the discussions in the Senate there was no great manifestation on the part of our Democratic friends in favor of reducing rates on necessities. They voted to maintain the tariff rates on everything that came from their particular sections. If we are to have free trade, certainly it cannot be had through the maintenance of Republican majorities in the Senate and House and a Republican administration.

THEODORE ROOSEVELT: THE NEW NATIONALISM (1910)

Source: *The New Nationalism*, New York, 1910, pp. 3–33.

I stand for the square deal. But when I say that I am for the square deal, I mean not merely that I stand for fair play under the present rules of the game but that I stand for having those rules changed so as to work for a more substantial equality of opportunity and of reward for equally good service. One word of warning, which, I think, is hardly necessary in Kansas. When I say I want a square deal for the poor man, I do not mean that I want a square deal for the man who remains poor because he has not got the energy to work for himself. If a man who has had a chance will not make good, then he has got to quit. And you men of the Grand Army, you want justice for the brave man who fought and punishment for the coward who shirked his work. Is not that so?

Now, this means that our government, national and state, must be freed from the sinister influence or control of special interests. … We must drive the special interests out of politics. That is one of our tasks today. Every special interest is entitled to justice—full, fair, and complete—and, now, mind you, if there were any attempt by mob violence to plunder and work harm to the special interest, whatever it may be, that I most dislike, and the wealthy man, whomsoever he may be, for whom I have the greatest contempt, I would fight for him, and you would if you were worth your salt. He should have justice. For every special interest is entitled to justice, but not one is entitled to a vote in Congress, to a voice on the bench, or to representation in any public office. The Constitution guarantees protection to property, and we must make that promise good. But it does not give the right of suffrage to any corporation.

The true friend of property, the true conservative, is he who insists that property shall be the servant and not the master of the commonwealth; who insists that the creature of man's making shall be the servant and not the master of the man who made it. The citizens of the United States must effectively control the mighty commercial forces which they have themselves called into being. There can be no effective control of corporations while their political activity remains. To put an end to it will be neither a short nor an easy task, but it can be done.

We must have complete and effective publicity of corporate affairs so that the people may know beyond peradventure whether the corporations obey the law and whether their management entitles them to the confidence of the public. It is necessary that laws should be passed to prohibit the use of corporate funds directly or indirectly for political purposes; it is still more necessary that such laws should be thoroughly enforced. Corporate expenditures for political purposes, and especially such expenditures by public service corporations, have supplied one of the principal sources of corruption in our political affairs.

It has become entirely clear that we must have government supervision of the capitalization, not only of public service corporations, including, particularly, railways, but of all corporations doing an interstate business. I do not wish to see the nation forced into the ownership of the railways if it can possibly be avoided, and the only alternative is thoroughgoing and effective regulation, which shall be based on a full knowledge of all the facts, including a physical valuation of property. This physical valuation is not needed, or, at least, is very rarely needed, for fixing rates; but it is needed as the basis of honest capitalization.

We have come to recognize that franchises should never be granted, except for a limited time, and never without proper provision for compensation to the public. It is my personal belief that the same kind and degree of control and supervision which should be exercised over public service corporations should be extended also to combinations which control necessaries of life, such as meat, oil, and coal, or which deal in them on an important scale. I have no doubt that the ordinary man who has control of them is much like ourselves. I have no doubt he would like to do well, but I want to have enough supervision to help him realize that desire to do well.

I believe that the officers, and, especially, the directors, of corporations should be held personally responsible when any corporation breaks the law.

Combinations in industry are the result of an imperative economic law which cannot be repealed by political legislation. The effort at prohibiting all combination has substantially failed. The way out lies, not in attempting to prevent such combinations but in completely controlling them in the interest of the public welfare. For that purpose the Federal Bureau of Corporations is an agency of first importance. Its powers, and, therefore, its efficiency, as well as that of the Interstate Commerce Commission, should be largely increased. We have a right to expect from the Bureau of Corporations and from the Interstate Commerce Commission a very high grade of public service. We should be as sure of the proper conduct of the interstate railways and the proper management of interstate business as we are now sure of the conduct and management of the national banks, and we should have as effective supervision in one case as in the other. The Hepburn Act, and the amendment to the act in the shape in which it finally passed Congress at the last session, represent a long step in advance, and we must go yet further.

There is a widespread belief among our people that, under the methods of making tariffs which have hitherto obtained, the special interests are too influential. Probably this is true of both the big special interests and the little special interests. These methods have put a premium on selfishness, and, naturally, the selfish big interests have gotten more than their smaller, though equally selfish, brothers. The duty of Congress is to provide a method by which the interest of the whole people shall be all that receives consideration. To this end there must be an expert tariff commission, wholly removed from the possibility of political pressure or of improper business influence. Such a commission can find the real difference between cost of production, which is mainly the difference of labor cost here and abroad. As fast as its recommendations are made, I believe in revising one schedule at a time. A general revision of the tariff almost inevitably leads to logrolling and the subordination of the general public interest to local and special interests.

The absence of effective state and, especially, national restraint upon unfair money getting has tended to create a small class of enormously wealthy and economically powerful men whose chief object is to hold and increase their power. The prime need is to change the conditions which enable these men to accumulate power which it is not for the general welfare that they should hold or exercise. We grudge no man a fortune which represents his own power and sagacity when exercised with entire regard to the welfare of his fellows.... We should permit it to be gained only so long as the gaining represents benefit to the community. This, I know, implies a policy of a far more active governmental interference with social and economic conditions in this country than we have yet had, but I think we have got to face the fact that such an increase in governmental control is now necessary.

No man should receive a dollar unless that dollar has been fairly earned. Every dollar received should represent a dollar's worth of service rendered—not gambling in stocks but service rendered. The really big fortune, the swollen fortune, by the mere fact of its size, acquires qualities which differentiate it in kind as well as in degree from what is possessed by men of relatively small means. Therefore, I believe in a graduated income tax on big fortunes, and in another tax which is far more easily collected and far more effective—a graduated inheritance tax on big fortunes, properly safeguarded against evasion and increasing rapidly in amount with the size of the estate.

The people of the United States suffer from periodical financial panics to a degree substantially unknown among the other nations which approach us in financial strength. There is no reason why we should suffer what they escape. It is of profound importance that our financial system should be promptly investigated and so thoroughly and effectively revised as to make it certain that hereafter our currency will no longer fail at critical times to meet our needs....

Nothing is more true than that excess of every kind is followed by reaction; a fact which should be pondered by reformer and reactionary alike. We are face to face with new conceptions of the relations of property to human welfare, chiefly because certain advocates of the rights of property as against the rights of men have been pushing their claims too far. The man who wrongly holds that every human right is secondary to his profit must now give way to the advocate of human welfare, who rightly maintains that every man holds his property subject to the general right of the community to regulate its use to whatever degree the public welfare may require it.

But I think we may go still further. The right to regulate the use of wealth in the public interest is universally admitted. Let us admit also the right to regulate the terms and conditions of labor, which is the chief element of wealth, directly in the interest of the common good. The fundamental thing to do for every man is to give him a chance to reach a place in which he will make the greatest possible contribution to the public welfare. Understand what I say there. Give him a chance, not push him up if he will not be pushed. Help any man who stumbles; if he lies down, it is a poor job to try to carry him; but if he is a worthy man, try your best to see that he gets a chance to show the worth that is in him.

No man can be a good citizen unless he has a wage more than sufficient to cover the bare cost of living and hours of labor short enough so that after his day's work is done he will have time and energy to bear his share in the management of the community, to help in carrying the general load. We keep countless men from being good citizens by the conditions of life with which we surround them. We need comprehensive workmen's compensation acts, both state and national laws to regulate child labor and work for women, and, especially, we need in our common schools not merely education in book learning but also practical training for daily life and work. We need to enforce better sanitary conditions for our workers and to extend the use of safety appliances for our workers in industry and commerce, both within and between the states. Also, friends, in the interest of the workingman himself we need to set our faces like flint against mob violence just as against corporate greed; against violence and injustice and lawlessness by wage workers just as much as against lawless cunning and greed and selfish arrogance of employers.

If I could ask but one thing of my fellow countrymen, my request would be that, whenever they go in for reform, they remember the two sides, and that they always exact justice from one side as much as from the other. I have small use for the public servant who can always see and denounce the corruption of the capitalist, but who cannot persuade himself, especially before election, to say a word about lawless mob violence. And I have equally small use for the man, be he a judge on the bench, or editor of a great paper, or wealthy and influential private citizen, who can see clearly enough and denounce the lawlessness of mob violence, but whose eyes are closed so that he is blind when the question is one of corruption in business on a gigantic scale....

I do not ask for overcentralization; but I do ask that we work in a spirit of broad and far-reaching nationalism when we work for what concerns our people as a whole. We are all Americans. Our common interests are as broad as the continent. I speak to you here in Kansas exactly as I would speak in New York or Georgia, for the most vital problems are those which affect us all alike. The national government belongs to the whole American people, and where the whole American people are interested, that interest can be guarded effectively only by the national government. The betterment which we seek must be accomplished, I believe, mainly through the national government.

The American people are right in demanding that New Nationalism, without which we cannot hope to deal with new problems. The New Nationalism puts the national need before sectional or personal advantage. It is impatient of the utter confusion that results from local legislatures attempting to treat national issues as local issues. It is still more impatient of the impotence which springs from overdivision of governmental powers, the impotence which makes it possible for local selfishness or for legal cunning, hired by wealthy special interests, to bring national activities to a deadlock. This New Nationalism regards the executive power as the steward of the public welfare. It demands of the judiciary that it shall be interested primarily in human welfare rather than in property, just as it demands that the representative body shall represent all the people rather than any one class or section of the people....

One of the fundamental necessities in a representative government such as ours is to make certain that the men to whom the people delegate their power shall serve the people by whom they are elected and not the special interests. I believe that every national officer, elected or appointed, should be forbidden to perform any service or receive any compensation, directly or indirectly, from interstate corporations; and a similar provision could not fail to be useful within the states.

The object of government is the welfare of the people. The material progress and prosperity of a nation are desirable chiefly so far as they lead to the moral and material welfare of all good citizens. Just in proportion as the average man and woman are honest, capable of sound judgment and high ideals, active in public affairs—but, first of all, sound in their homelife, and the father and mother of healthy children whom they bring up well—just so far, and no farther, we may count our civilization a success. We must have—I believe we have already—a genuine and permanent moral awakening, without which no wisdom of legislation or administration really means anything; and, on the other hand, we must try to secure the social and economic legislation without which any improvement due to purely moral agitation is necessarily evanescent.

WOODROW WILSON: FIRST INAUGURAL ADDRESS (1913)

Source: *Congressional Record*, Washington, 63 Cong., 1 Sess., pp. 2–3.

There has been a change of government. It began two years ago, when the House of Representatives became Democratic by a decisive majority. It has now been completed. The Senate about to assemble will also be Democratic. The offices of President and Vice-President have been put into the hands of Democrats. What does the change mean? That is the question that is uppermost in our minds today. That is the question I am going to try to answer in order, if I may, to interpret the occasion.

It means much more than the mere success of a party. The success of a party means little except when the nation is using that party for a large and definite purpose. No one can mistake the purpose for which the nation now seeks to use the Democratic Party. It seeks to use it to interpret a change in its own plans and point of view. Some old things with which we had grown familiar, and which had begun to creep into the very habit of our thought and of our lives, have altered their aspect as we have latterly looked critically upon them with fresh, awakened eyes; have dropped their disguises and shown themselves alien and sinister. Some new things, as we look frankly upon them, willing to comprehend their real character, have come to assume the aspect of things long believed in and familiar, stuff of our own convictions. We have been refreshed by a new insight into our own life.

We see that in many things that life is very great. It is incomparably great in its material aspects, in its body of wealth, in the diversity and sweep of its energy, in the industries which have been conceived and built up by the genius of individual men and the limitless enterprise of groups of men. It is great, also, very great, in its moral force. Nowhere else in the world have noble men and women exhibited in more striking forms the beauty and the energy of sympathy and helpfulness and counsel in their efforts to rectify wrong, alleviate suffering, and set the weak in the way of strength and hope. We have built up, moreover, a great system of government, which has stood through a long age as in many respects a model for those who seek to set liberty upon foundations that will endure against fortuitous change, against storm and accident. Our life contains every great thing, and contains it in rich abundance.

But the evil has come with the good, and much fine gold has been corroded. With riches has come inexcusable waste. We have squandered a great part of what we might have used and have not stopped to conserve the exceeding bounty of nature, without which our genius for enterprise would have been worthless and impotent, scorning to be careful, shamefully prodigal as well as admirably efficient. We have been proud of our industrial achievements, but we have not hitherto stopped thoughtfully enough to count the human cost, the cost of lives snuffed out, of energies overtaxed and broken, the fearful physical and spiritual cost to the men and women and children upon whom the dead weight and burden of it all has fallen pitilessly the years through. The groans and agony of it all had not yet reached our ears, the solemn, moving undertone of our life, coming up out of the mines and factories and out of every home where the struggle had its intimate and familiar seat. With the great government went many deep secret things which we too long delayed to look into and scrutinize with candid, fearless eyes. The great government we loved has too often been made use of for private and selfish purposes, and those who used it had forgotten the people.

At last a vision has been vouchsafed us of our life as a whole. We see the bad with the good, the debased and decadent with the sound and vital. With this vision we approach new affairs. Our duty is to cleanse, to reconsider, to restore, to correct the evil without impairing the good, to purify and humanize every process of our common life without weakening or sentimentalizing it.

There has been something crude and heartless and unfeeling in our haste to succeed and be great. Our thought has been "Let every man look out for himself, let every generation look out for itself," while we reared giant machinery which made it impossible that any but those who stood at the levers of control should have a chance to look out for themselves. We had not forgotten our morals. We

remembered well enough that we had set up a policy which was meant to serve the humblest as well as the most powerful, with an eye single to the standards of justice and fair play, and remembered it with pride. But we were very heedless and in a hurry to be great.

We have come now to the sober second thought. The scales of heedlessness have fallen from our eyes. We have made up our minds to square every process of our national life again with the standards we so proudly set up at the beginning and have always carried at our hearts. Our work is a work of restoration.

We have itemized with some degree of particularity the things that ought to be altered and here are some of the chief items; a tariff which cuts us off from our proper part in the commerce of the world, violates the just principles of taxation, and makes the government a facile instrument in the hands of private interests; a banking and currency system based upon the necessity of the government to sell its bonds fifty years ago and perfectly adapted to concentrating cash and restricting credits; an industrial system which, take it on all its sides, financial as well as administrative, holds capital in leading strings, restricts the liberties and limits the opportunities of labor, and exploits without renewing or conserving the natural resources of the country; a body of agricultural activities never yet given the efficiency of great business undertakings or served as it should be through the instrumentality of science taken directly to the farm, or afforded the facilities of credit best suited to its practical needs; watercourses undeveloped, waste places unreclaimed, forests untended, fast disappearing without plan or prospect of renewal, unregarded waste heaps at every mine.

We have studied, as perhaps no other nation has, the most effective means of production, but we have not studied cost or economy as we should either as organizers of industry, as statesmen, or as individuals. Nor have we studied and perfected the means by which government may be put at the service of humanity, in safeguarding the health of the nation, the health of its men and its women and its children, as well as their rights in the struggle for existence.

This is no sentimental duty. The firm basis of government is justice, not pity. These are matters of justice. There can be no equality of opportunity, the first essential of justice in the body politic, if men and women and children be not shielded in their lives, their very vitality, from the consequences of great industrial and social processes which they cannot alter, control, or singly cope with. Society must see to it that it does not itself crush or weaken or damage its own constituent parts. The first duty of law is to keep sound the society it serves. Sanitary laws, pure-food laws, and laws determining conditions of labor which individuals are powerless to determine for themselves are intimate parts of the very business of justice and legal efficiency.

These are some of the things we ought to do, and not leave the others undone, the old-fashioned, never-to-be-neglected, fundamental safeguarding of property and of individual right. This is the high enterprise of the new day: to lift everything that concerns our life as a nation to the light that shines from the hearthfire of every man's conscience and vision of the right. It is inconceivable that we should do this as partisans; it is inconceivable we should do it in ignorance of the facts as they are or in blind haste.

We shall restore, not destroy. We shall deal with our economic system as it is and as it may be modified, not as it might be if we had a clean sheet of paper to write upon; and step by step we shall make it what it should be, in the spirit of those who question their own wisdom and seek counsel and knowledge, not shallow self-satisfaction or the excitement of excursions whither they cannot tell. Justice, and only justice, shall always be our motto.

And yet it will be no cool process of mere science. The nation has been deeply stirred, stirred by a solemn passion, stirred by the knowledge of wrong, of ideals lost, of government too often debauched and made an instrument of evil. The feelings with which we face this new age of right and opportunity sweep across our heartstrings like some air out of God's own presence, where justice and mercy are reconciled and the judge and the brother are one. We know our task to be no mere task of politics but a task which shall search us through and through, whether we be able to understand our time and the need of our people, whether we be indeed their spokesmen and interpreters, whether we have the pure heart to comprehend and the rectified will to choose our high course of action.

This is not a day of triumph; it is a day of dedication. Here muster, not the forces of party but the forces of humanity. Men's hearts wait upon us; men's lives hang in the balance; men's hopes call upon us to say what we will do. Who shall live up to the great trust? Who dares fail to try? I summon all honest men, all patriotic, all forward-looking men, to my side. God helping me, I will not fail them, if they will but counsel and sustain me!

LOUIS D. BRANDEIS: THE MONEY TRUST (1913)

Source: *Harper's Weekly*, Nov. 22, 1913: "Breaking the Money Trust."

The dominant element in our financial oligarchy is the investment banker. Associated banks, trust companies, and life insurance companies are his tools. Controlled railroads, public-service and industrial corporations are his subjects. Though properly but middlemen, these bankers bestride as masters America's business world, so that practically no large enterprise can be undertaken successfully without their participation or approval. These bankers are, of course, able men possessed of large fortunes; but the most potent factor in their control of business is not the possession of extraordinary ability or huge wealth. The key to their power is combination—concentration, intensive and comprehensive—advancing on three distinct lines:

First, there is the obvious consolidation of banks and trust companies; the less obvious affiliations—through stockholdings, voting trusts, and interlocking directorates—of banking institutions which are not legally connected; and the joint transactions, gentlemen's agreements, and "banking ethics" which eliminate competition among the investment bankers.

Second, there is the consolidation of railroads into huge systems, the large combinations of public-service corporations and the formation of industrial trusts, which, by making business so "big" that local, independent banking concerns cannot alone supply the necessary funds, has created dependence upon the associated New York bankers.

But combination, however intensive, along these lines only, could not have produced the money trust—another and more potent factor of combination was added.

Third, investment bankers, like J. P. Morgan & Co., dealers in bonds, stocks, and notes, encroached upon the functions of the three other classes of corporations with which their business brought them into contact. They became the directing power in railroads, public-service and industrial companies through which our great business operations are conducted—the makers of bonds and stocks. They became the directing power in the life insurance companies and other corporate reservoirs of the people's savings—the buyers of bonds and stocks. They became the directing power also in banks and trust companies—the depositaries of the quick capital of the country—the lifeblood of business, with which they and others carried on their operations. Thus, four distinct functions, each essential to business, and each exercised, originally, by a distinct set of men, became united in the investment banker. It is to this union of business functions that the existence of the money trust is mainly due.

The development of our financial oligarchy followed, in this respect, lines with which the history of political despotism has familiarized us—usurpation, proceeding by gradual encroachment rather than by violent acts; subtle and often long-concealed concentration of distinct functions, which are beneficent when separately administered and dangerous only when combined in the same persons. It was by processes such as these that Caesar Augustus became master of Rome. The makers of our own Constitution had in mind like dangers to our political liberty when they provided so carefully for the separation of governmental powers.

The original function of the investment banker was that of dealer in bonds, stocks, and notes; buying mainly at wholesale from corporations, municipalities, states, and governments which need money, and selling to those seeking investments. The banker performs, in this respect, the function of a merchant; and the function is a very useful one. Large business enterprises are conducted generally by corporations. The permanent capital of corporations is represented by bonds and stocks. The bonds and stocks of the more important corporations are owned, in large part, by small investors, who do not participate in the management of the company. Corporations require the aid of a banker-middleman, for they lack generally the reputation and clientele essential to selling their own bonds and stocks direct to the investor. Investors in corporate securities also require the services of a banker-middleman.

The number of securities upon the market is very large. Only a part of these securities is listed on the New York Stock Exchange; but its listings alone comprise about 1,600 different issues aggregating about $26.5 billion, and each year new listings are made averaging about 233, to an amount of $1.5 billion. For a small investor to make an intelligent selection from these many corporate securities—indeed, to pass an intelligent judgment upon a single one—is ordinarily impossible. He lacks the ability, the facilities, the training, and the time essential to a proper investigation. Unless his purchase is to be little better than a gamble, he needs the advice of an expert, who, combining special knowledge with judgment, has the facilities and incentive to make a thorough investigation.

This dependence, both of corporations and investors, upon the banker has grown in recent years, since women and others who do not participate in the management, have become the owners of so large a part of the stocks and bonds of our great corporations. Over half of the stockholders of the American Sugar Refining

Company and nearly half of the stock-holders of the Pennsylvania Railroad and of the New York, New Haven & Hartford Railroad are women.

Goodwill—the possession by a dealer of numerous and valuable regular customers—is always an important element in merchandising. But in the business of selling bonds and stocks, it is of exceptional value, for the very reason that the small investor relies so largely upon the banker's judgment. This confidential relation of the banker to customers—and the knowledge of the customers' private affairs acquired incidentally, is often a determining factor in the marketing of securities. With the advent of big business, such goodwill possessed by the older banking houses, preeminently J. P. Morgan & Co. and their Philadelphia house called Drexel & Co., by Lee, Higginson & Co. and Kidder, Peabody, & Co. of Boston, and by Kuhn, Loeb & Co. of New York, became of enhanced importance. The volume of new security issues was greatly increased by huge railroad consolidations, the development of the holding companies, and particularly by the formation of industrial trusts. The rapidly accumulating savings of our people sought investment. The field of operations for the dealer in securities was thus much enlarged. And, as the securities were new and untried, the services of the investment banker were in great demand, and his powers and profits increased accordingly.

But this enlargement of their legitimate field of operations did not satisfy investment bankers. They were not content merely to deal in securities. They desired to manufacture them also, and became promoters or allied themselves with promoters. Thus it was that J. P. Morgan & Company formed the steel trust, the Harvester trust, and the shipping trust. And, adding the duties of undertaker to those of midwife, the investment bankers became in times of corporate disaster, members of the security-holders' "Protective Committees"; then they participated as "Reorganization Managers" in the reincarnation of the unsuccessful corporations and ultimately became directors.

It was in this way that the Morgan associates acquired their hold upon the Southern Railway, the Northern Pacific, the Reading, the Erie, the Père Marquette, the Chicago and Great Western, and the Cincinnati, Hamilton & Dayton. Often they insured the continuance of that control by the device of the voting trust; but even where no voting trust was created, a secure hold was acquired upon reorganization. It was in this way also that Kuhn, Loeb & Co. became potent in the Union Pacific and the Baltimore & Ohio.

But the banker's participation in the management of the corporations was not limited to cases of promotion or reorganization. An urgent or extensive need of new money was considered a sufficient reason for the banker's entering a board of directors. And often without even such excuse the investment banker has secured a place upon the Board of Directors, through his powerful influence or the control of his customers' proxies. Such seems to have been the fatal entrance of Mr. Morgan into the management of the then prosperous New York, New Haven & Hartford Railroad in 1892. And when once a banker has entered the Board—whatever may have been the occasion—his grip proves tenacious and his influence usually supreme, for he controls the supply of new money.

The investment banker is naturally on the lookout for good bargains in bonds and stocks. Like other merchants, he wants to buy his merchandise cheap. But, when he becomes director of a corporation, he occupies a position which prevents the transaction by which he acquires its corporate securities from being properly called a bargain. Can there be real bargaining where the same man is on both sides of a trade? The investment banker, through his controlling influence on the Board of Directors, decides that the corporation shall issue and sell the securities, decides the price at which it shall sell them, and decides that it shall sell the securities to himself. The fact that there are other directors besides the banker on the Board does not, in practice, prevent this being the result. The banker, who holds the purse strings, becomes usually the dominant spirit.

Through voting trusteeships, exclusive financial agencies, membership on executive or finance committees, or by mere directorships, J. P. Morgan & Co. and their associates, hold such financial power in at least thirty-two transportation systems, public-utility corporations,

and industrial companies—companies with an aggregate capitalization of $17,273,000,000. Mainly for corporations so controlled, J. P. Morgan & Co. procured the public marketing in ten years of security issues aggregating $1,950,000,000. This huge sum does not include any issues marketed privately nor any issues, however marketed, of intrastate corporations. Kuhn, Loeb & Co. and a few other investment bankers exercise similar control over many other corporations.

Such control of railroads, public-service and industrial corporations assures to the investment bankers an ample supply of securities at attractive prices; and merchandise well bought is half-sold. But these bond and stock merchants are not disposed to take even a slight risk as to their ability to market their goods. They saw that if they could control the security buyers, as well as the security makers, investment banking would, indeed, be "a happy hunting ground"; and they have made it so.

The numerous small investors cannot, in the strict sense, be controlled; but their dependence upon the banker insures their being duly influenced. A large part, however, of all bonds issued and of many stocks are bought by the prominent corporate investors; and most prominent among these are the life insurance companies, the trust companies, and the banks. The purchase of a security by these institutions not only relieves the banker of the merchandise but recommends it strongly to the small investor, who believes that these institutions are wisely managed. These controlled corporate investors are not only large customers, but may be particularly accommodating ones. Individual investors are moody. They buy only when they want to do so. They are sometimes inconveniently reluctant. Corporate investors, if controlled, may be made to buy when the bankers need a market. It was natural that the investment bankers proceeded to get control of the great life insurance companies, as well as of the trust companies and the banks.

The field thus occupied is uncommonly rich. The life insurance companies are our leading institutions for savings. Their huge surplus and reserves, augmented daily, are always clamoring for investment. No panic or money shortage stops the inflow of new money from the perennial stream of premiums on existing policies and interest on existing investments. The three great companies—the New York Life, the Mutual of New York, and the Equitable—would have over $55 million of new money to invest annually even if they did not issue a single new policy.

In 1904—just before the Armstrong investigation—these three companies had together $1,247,331,738.18 of assets. They had issued in that year $1,025,671,126 of new policies. The New York legislature placed in 1906 certain restrictions upon their growth; so that their new business since has averaged $547,384,212, or only 53 percent of what it was in 1904. But the aggregate assets of these companies increased in the last eight years

to $1,817,052,260.36. At the time of the Armstrong investigation the average age of these three companies was fifty-six years. The growth of assets in the last eight years was about half as large as the total growth in the preceding fifty-six years. These three companies must invest annually about $70 million of new money; and, besides, many old investments expire or are changed and the proceeds must be reinvested. A large part of all life insurance surplus and reserves are invested in bonds. The aggregate bond investments of these three companies on Jan. 1, 1913, was $1,019,153,268.93.

It was natural that the investment bankers should seek to control these never failing reservoirs of capital. George W. Perkins was vice-president of the New York Life, the largest of the companies. While remaining such he was made a partner in J. P. Morgan & Co., and in the four years preceding the Armstrong investigation, his firm sold the New York Life $38,804,918.51 in securities. The New York is a mutual company, supposed to be controlled by its policyholders. But "the so-called control of life insurance companies by policyholders through mutualization is a farce" and "its only result is to keep in office a self-constituted, self-perpetuating management."

The Equitable Life Assurance Society is a stock company and is controlled by $100,000 of stock. The dividend on this stock is limited by law to 7 percent; but in 1910 Mr. Morgan paid about $3 million for $51,000, par value of this stock, or $5,882.35 a share. The dividend return on the stock investment is less than one-eighth of one percent; but the assets controlled amount now to over $500 million. And certain of these assets had an especial value for investment bankers; namely, the large holdings of stock in banks and trust companies.

The Armstrong investigation disclosed the extent of financial power exerted through the insurance company holdings of bank and trust company stock. The committee recommended legislation compelling the insurance companies to dispose of the stock within five years. A law to that effect was enacted, but the time was later extended. The companies then disposed of a part of their bank and trust company stocks; but, being controlled by the investment bankers, these gentlemen sold the bank and trust company stocks to themselves.

The banks and trust companies are depositaries, in the main, not of the people's savings but of the businessman's quick capital. Yet, since the investment banker acquired control of banks and trust companies, these institutions also have become, like the life companies, large purchasers of bonds and stocks. Many of our national banks have invested in this manner a large part of all their resources, including capital, surplus, and deposits. The bond investments of some banks exceed by far the aggregate of their capital and surplus and nearly equal their loanable deposits.

The goose that lays golden eggs has been considered a most valuable possession. But even more profitable is the privilege of taking the golden eggs laid by somebody else's goose. The investment bankers and their associates now enjoy that privilege. They control the people through the people's own money. If the bankers' power were commensurate only with their wealth, they would have relatively little influence on American business. Vast fortunes like those of the Astors are no doubt regrettable. They are inconsistent with democracy. They are unsocial. And they seem peculiarly unjust when they represent largely unearned increment. But the wealth of the Astors does not endanger political or industrial liberty. It is insignificant in amount as compared with the aggregate wealth of America, or even of New York City. It lacks significance largely because its owners have only the income from their own wealth. The Astor wealth is static.

The wealth of the Morgan associates is dynamic. The power and the growth of power of our financial oligarchs comes from wielding the savings and quick capital of others. In two of the three great life insurance companies the influence of J. P. Morgan & Co. and their associates is exerted without any individual investment by them whatsoever. Even in the Equitable, where Mr. Morgan bought an actual majority of all the outstanding stock, his investment amounts to little more than one-half of one percent of the assets of the company. The fetters which bind the people are forged from the people's own gold.

But the reservoir of other people's money, from which the investment bankers now draw their greatest power, is not the life insurance companies but the banks and the trust companies. Bank deposits represent the really quick capital of the nation. They are the lifeblood of businesses. Their effective force is much greater than that of an equal amount of wealth permanently invested. The thirty-four banks and trust companies, which the Pujo Committee declared to be directly controlled by the Morgan associates, held $1,983,000,000 in deposits. Control of these institutions means the ability to lend a large part of these funds, directly and indirectly, to themselves; and what is often even more important, the power to prevent the funds being lent to any rival interests. These huge deposits can, in the discretion of those in control, be used to meet the temporary needs of their subject corporations. When bonds and stocks are issued to finance permanently these corporations, the bank deposits, can in large part be loaned by the investment bankers in control to themselves and their associates, so that the securities may be carried by them until sold to investors. Or these bank deposits may be loaned to allied bankers or jobbers in securities or to speculators, to enable them to carry the bonds or stocks.

Easy money tends to make securities rise in the market. Tight money nearly always makes them fall. The control by the leading investment bankers over the banks and trust companies is so great, that they can often determine for a time the market for money by lending or refusing to lend on the Stock Exchange. In this way, among others, they have power to affect the general trend of prices in bonds and stocks. Their power over a particular security is even greater. Its sale on the market may depend upon whether the security is favored or discriminated against when offered to the banks and trust companies, as collateral for loans.

Furthermore, it is the investment banker's access to other people's money in controlled banks and trust companies which alone enables any individual banking concern to take so large [a] part of the annual output of bonds and stocks. The banker's own capital, however large, would soon be exhausted. And even the loanable funds of the banks would often be exhausted but for the large deposits made in those banks by the life insurance, railroad, public-service, and industrial corporations which the bankers also control. On December 31, 1912, the three leading life insurance companies had deposits in banks and trust companies aggregating $13,839,189.08. As the Pujo Committee finds:

> The men, who through their control over the funds of our railroads and industrial companies are able to direct where such funds shall be kept and thus to create these great reservoirs of the people's money, are the ones who are in position to tap those reservoirs for the ventures in which they are interested and to prevent their being tapped for purposes of which they do not approve.

The latter is quite as important a factor as the former. It is the controlling consideration in its effect on competition in the railroad and industrial world.

But the power of the investment banker over other people's money is often more direct and effective than that exerted through controlled banks and trust companies. J. P. Morgan & Co. achieve the supposedly impossible feat of having their cake and eating it too. They buy the bonds and stocks of controlled railroads and industrial concerns and pay the purchase price; and still do not part with their money. This is accomplished by the simple device of becoming the bank of deposit of the controlled corporations, instead of having the company deposit in some merely controlled bank in whose operation others have at least some share. When J. P. Morgan & Co. buy an issue of securities, the purchase money, instead of being paid over to the corporation, is retained by the banker for the corporation, to be drawn upon only as the funds are needed by the corporation. And as the securities are issued in large blocks, and the money raised is often not all spent until long thereafter, the aggregate of the balances remaining in the banker's hands are huge. Thus J. P. Morgan & Co. (including their Philadelphia house, called Drexel & Co.) held on November 1, 1912, deposits aggregating $162,491,819.65.

The operations of so comprehensive a system of concentration necessarily developed in the bankers overweening power. And the bankers' power grows by what it feeds on. Power begets wealth; and added wealth opens ever new opportunities for the acquisition of wealth and power. The operations of these bankers are so vast and numerous that even a very reasonable compensation for the service performed by the bankers, would, in the aggregate, produce for them incomes so large as to result in huge accumulations of capital. But the compensation taken by the bankers as commissions or profits is far from reasonable. Occupying, as they so frequently do, the inconsistent position of being at the same time seller and buyer, the standard for so-called compensation actually applied is not the "rule of reason" but "all the traffic will bear." And this is true even where there is no sinister motive. The weakness of human nature prevents men from being good judges of their own deservings.

The syndicate formed by J. P. Morgan & Co. to underwrite the United States Steel Corporation took for their services securities which netted $62.5 million in cash. Of this huge sum J. P. Morgan & Co. received, as syndicate managers, $12.5 million in addition to the share which they were entitled to receive as syndicate members. This sum of $62.5 million was only a part of the fees paid for the service of monopolizing the steel industry. In addition to the commissions taken specifically for organizing the United States Steel Corporation, large sums were paid for organizing the several companies of which it is composed. For instance, the

National Tube Company was capitalized at $80 million of stock, $40 million of which was common stock. Half of this $40 million was taken by J. P. Morgan & Co. and associates for promotion services; and the $20 million stock so taken became later exchangeable into $25 million of Steel Common. Commissioner of Corporations Herbert Knox Smith found that:

More than $150 million of the stock of the Steel Corporation was issued directly or indirectly (through exchange) for mere promotion or underwriting services. In other words, nearly one-seventh of the total capital stock of the Steel Corporation appears to have been issued directly or indirectly to promoters' services.

The so-called fees and commissions taken by the bankers and associates upon the organization of the trusts have been exceptionally large. But even after the trusts are successfully launched the exactions of the bankers are often extortionate. The syndicate which underwrote, in 1901, the Steel Corporation's preferred stock conversion plan, advanced only $20 million in cash and received an underwriting commission of $6.8 million.

The exaction of huge commissions is not confined to trust and other industrial concerns. The Interborough Railway is a most prosperous corporation. It earned last year nearly 21 percent on its capital stock, and secured from New York City, in connection with the subway extension, a very favorable contract. But when it financed its $170 million bond issue, it was agreed that J. P. Morgan & Co. should receive 3 percent, that is, $5.1 million, for forming this syndicate.

More recently, the New York, New Haven & Hartford Railroad agreed to pay J. P. Morgan & Co. a commission of $1,680,000, that is, 2½ percent, to form a syndicate to underwrite an issue at par of $67 million twenty-year 6 percent convertible debentures. That means: the bankers bound themselves to take at 97½ any of these 6 percent convertible bonds which stockholders might be unwilling to buy at 100. When the contract was made the New Haven's then outstanding 6 percent convertible bonds were selling at 114. And the new issue, as soon as announced, was in such demand that the public offered and has ever since been willing to buy at 106—bonds which the company were to pay J. P. Morgan & Co. $1,680,000 to be willing to take at par.

These large profits from promotions, underwritings and security purchases led to a revolutionary change in the conduct of our leading banking institutions. It was obvious that control by the investment bankers of the deposits in banks and trust companies was an essential element in their securing these huge profits. And the bank officers naturally asked, "Why then should not the banks and trust companies share in so profitable a field? Why should not they themselves become investment bankers, too, with all the new functions incident to 'big business'?" To do so would involve a departure from the legitimate sphere of the banking business—which is the making of temporary loans to other business concerns.

But the temptation was irresistible. The invasion of the investment banker into the banks' field of operation was followed by a counterinvasion by the banks into the realm of the investment banker. And most prominent among the banks were the National City and the First National of New York. But theirs was not a hostile invasion. The contending forces met as allies, joined forces to control the business of the country and to "divide the spoils." The alliance was cemented by voting trusts, by interlocking directorates, and by joint ownerships. There resulted the fullest "cooperation"; and more railroads, public-service corporations, and great industrial concerns were brought into complete subjection.

WOODROW WILSON: THE TAMPICO AFFAIR (1914)

Source: [United States Department of State] *Papers Relating to Foreign Relations of the United States*, Washington, 1914, pp. 474–476.

It is my duty to call your attention to a situation which has arisen in our dealings with General Victoriano Huerta at Mexico City which calls for action, and to ask your advice and cooperation in acting upon it.

On the 9th of April a paymaster of the U.S.S. *Dolphin* landed at the Iturbide Bridge landing at Tampico with a whaleboat and boat's crew to take off certain supplies needed by his ship, and while engaged in loading the boat was arrested by an officer and squad of men of the army of General Huerta. Neither the paymaster nor anyone of the boat's crew was armed. Two of the men were in the boat when the arrest took place and were obliged to leave it and submit to be taken into custody, notwithstanding the fact that the boat carried, both at her bow and at her stern, the flag of the United States.

The officer who made the arrest was proceeding up one of the streets of the town with his prisoners when met by an officer of higher authority, who ordered him to return to the landing and await orders; and within an hour and a half from the time of the arrest, orders were received from the commander of the Huertista forces at Tampico for the release of the paymaster and his men. The release was followed by apologies from the commander and later by an expression of regret by General Huerta himself.

General Huerta urged that martial law obtained at the time at Tampico; that orders had been issued that no one should be allowed to land at the Iturbide Bridge; and that our sailors had no right to land there. Our naval commanders at the port had not been notified of any such prohibition; and, even if they had been, the only justifiable course open to the local authorities would have been to request the paymaster and his crew to withdraw and to lodge a protest with the commanding officer of the fleet. Admiral

Mayo regarded the arrest as so serious an affront that he was not satisfied with the apologies offered, but demanded that the flag of the United States be saluted with special ceremony by the military commander of the port.

The incident cannot be regarded as a trivial one, especially as two of the men arrested were taken from the boat itself—that is to say, from the territory of the United States—but had it stood by itself it might have been attributed to the ignorance or arrogance of a single officer. Unfortunately, it was not an isolated case. A series of incidents have recently occurred which cannot but create the impression that the representatives of General Huerta were willing to go out of their way to show disregard for the dignity and rights of this government and felt perfectly safe in doing what they pleased, making free to show in many ways their irritation and contempt.

A few days after the incident at Tampico, an orderly from the U.S.S. *Minnesota* was arrested at Vera Cruz while ashore in uniform to obtain the ship's mail and was for a time thrown into jail. An official dispatch from this government to its embassy at Mexico City was withheld by the authorities of the telegraphic service until peremptorily demanded by our chargé d'affaires in person. So far as I can learn, such wrongs and annoyances have been suffered to occur only against representatives of the United States. I have heard of no complaints from other governments of similar treatment.

Subsequent explanations and formal apologies did not and could not alter the popular impression, which it is possible it had been the object of the Huertista authorities to create, that the government of the United States was being singled out, and might be singled out with impunity, for slights and affronts in retaliation for its refusal to recognize the pretensions of General Huerta to be regarded as the constitutional provisional president of the Republic of Mexico.

The manifest danger of such a situation was that such offenses might grow from bad to worse until something happened of so gross and intolerable a sort as to lead directly and inevitably to armed conflict. It was necessary that the apologies of General Huerta and his representatives should go much further, that they should be such as to attract the attention of the whole population to their significance, and such as to impress upon General Huerta himself the necessity of seeing to it that no further occasion for explanations and professed regrets should arise.

I, therefore, felt it my duty to sustain Admiral Mayo in the whole of his demand and to insist that the flag of the United States should be saluted in such a way as to indicate a new spirit and attitude on the part of the Huertistas. Such a salute General Huerta has refused, and I have come to ask your approval and support in the course I now purpose to pursue.

This government can, I earnestly hope, in no circumstances be forced into war with the people of Mexico. Mexico is torn by civil strife. If we are to accept the tests of its own constitution, it has no government. General Huerta has set his power up in the City of Mexico, such as it is, without right and by methods for which there can be no justification. Only part of the country is under his control. If armed conflict should unhappily come as a result of his attitude of personal resentment toward this government, we should be fighting only General Huerta and those who adhere to him and give him their support, and our object would be only to restore to the people of the distracted republic the opportunity to set up again their own laws and their own government.

But I earnestly hope that war is not now in question. I believe that I speak for the American people when I say that we do not desire to control in any degree the affairs of our sister republic. Our feeling for the people of Mexico is one of deep and genuine friendship, and everything that we have so far done or refrained from doing has proceeded from our desire to help them, not to hinder or embarrass them. We would not wish even to exercise the good offices of friendship without their welcome and consent. The people of Mexico are entitled to settle their own domestic affairs in their own way, and we sincerely desire to respect their right. The present situation need have none of the grave implications of interference if we deal with it promptly, firmly, and wisely.

No doubt I could do what is necessary in the circumstances to enforce respect for our government without recourse to the Congress and yet not exceed my constitutional powers as President; but I do not wish to act in a matter possibly of so grave consequence except in close conference and cooperation with both the Senate and House. I, therefore, come to ask your approval that I should use the armed forces of the United States in such ways and to such an extent as may be necessary to obtain from General Huerta and his adherents the fullest recognition of the rights and dignity of the United States, even amidst the distressing conditions now unhappily obtaining in Mexico.

There can in what we do be no thought of aggression or of selfish aggrandizement. We seek to maintain the dignity and authority of the United States only because we wish always to keep our great influence unimpaired for the uses of liberty, both in the United States and wherever else it may be employed for the benefit of mankind.

WILLIAM JENNINGS BRYAN: AMERICAN PROTEST OVER THE SINKING OF THE *LUSITANIA* (1915)

Source: [United States Department of State] *Papers Relating to Foreign Relations of the United States*, Washington, 1915, Supplement: *The World War*, pp. 393–396.

Please call on the minister of foreign affairs and, after reading to him this communication, leave him with a copy.

In view of recent acts of the German authorities in violation of American rights on the high seas which culminated in the torpedoing and sinking of the British steamship *Lusitania* on May 7, 1915, by which over 100 American citizens lost their lives, it is clearly wise and desirable that the government of the United States and the Imperial German government should come to a clear and full understanding as to the grave situation which has resulted.

The sinking of the British passenger steamer *Falaba* by a German submarine on March 28, through which Leon C. Thrasher, an American citizen, was drowned; the attack on April 28 on the American vessel *Cushing* by a German aeroplane; the torpedoing on May 1 of the American vessel *Gulflight* by a German submarine, as a result of which two or more American citizens met their death; and, finally, the torpedoing and sinking of the steamship *Lusitania* constitute a series of events which the government of the United States has observed with growing concern, distress, and amazement.

Recalling the humane and enlightened attitude hitherto assumed by the Imperial German government in matters of international right, and particularly with regard to the freedom of the seas; having learned to recognize the German views and the German influence in the field of international obligation as always engaged upon the side of justice and humanity; and having understood the instructions of the Imperial German government to its naval commanders to be

upon the same plane of humane action prescribed by the naval codes of other nations, the government of the United States was loath to believe—it cannot now bring itself to believe—that these acts, so absolutely contrary to the rules, the practices, and the spirit of modern warfare, could have the countenance or sanction of that great government. It feels it to be its duty, therefore, to address the Imperial German government concerning them with the utmost frankness and in the earnest hope that it is not mistaken in expecting action on the part of the Imperial German government which will correct the unfortunate impressions which have been created and vindicate once more the position of that government with regard to the sacred freedom of the seas.

The government of the United States has been apprised that the Imperial German government considered themselves to be obliged by the extraordinary circumstances of the present war and the measures adopted by their adversaries in seeking to cut Germany off from all commerce, to adopt methods of retaliation which go much beyond the ordinary methods of warfare at sea, in the proclamation of a war zone from which they have warned neutral ships to keep away. This government has already taken occasion to inform the Imperial German government that it cannot admit the adoption of such measures or such a warning of danger to operate as in any degree an abbreviation of the rights of American ship-masters or of American citizens bound on lawful errands as passengers on merchant ships of belligerent nationality; and that it must hold the Imperial German government to a strict accountability for any infringement of those rights, intentional or incidental.

It does not understand the Imperial German government to question those rights. It assumes, on the contrary, that the Imperial government accept, as of course, the rule that the lives of noncombatants, whether they be of neutral citizenship or citizens of one of the nations at war, cannot lawfully or rightfully be put in jeopardy by the capture or destruction of an unarmed merchantman, and recognize also, as all other nations do, the obligation to take the usual precaution of visit and search to ascertain whether a suspected merchantman is in fact of belligerent nationality or is in fact carrying contraband of war under a neutral flag.

The government of the United States, therefore, desires to call the attention of the Imperial German government, with the utmost earnestness, to the fact that the objection to their present method of attack against the trade of their enemies lies in the practical impossibility of employing submarines in the destruction of commerce without disregarding those rules of fairness, reason, justice, and humanity which all modern opinion regards as imperative. It is practically impossible for the officers of a submarine to visit a merchantman at sea and examine her papers and cargo. It is practically impossible for them to make a prize of her; and, if they cannot put a

prize crew on board of her, they cannot sink her without leaving her crew and all on board of her to the mercy of the sea in her small boats.

These facts it is understood the Imperial German government frankly admit. We are informed that in the instances of which we have spoken time enough for even that poor measure of safety was not given, and, in at least two of the cases cited, not so much as a warning was received. Manifestly, submarines cannot be used against merchantmen, as the last few weeks have shown, without an inevitable violation of many sacred principles of justice and humanity.

American citizens act within their indisputable rights in taking their ships and in traveling wherever their legitimate business calls them upon the high seas, and exercise those rights in what should be the well-justified confidence that their lives will not be endangered by acts done in clear violation of universally acknowledged international obligations, and certainly in the confidence that their own government will sustain them in the exercise of their rights.

There was recently published in the newspapers of the United States, I regret to inform the Imperial German government, a formal warning, purporting to come from the Imperial German Embassy at Washington, addressed to the people of the United States, and stating, in effect, that any citizen of the United States who exercised his right of free travel upon the seas would do so at his peril if his journey should take him within the zone of waters within which the Imperial German Navy was using submarines against the commerce of Great Britain and France, notwithstanding the respectful but very earnest protests of his government, the government of the United States. I do not refer to this for the purpose of calling the attention of the Imperial German government at this time to the surprising irregularity of a communication from the Imperial German Embassy at Washington addressed to the people of the United States through the newspapers, but only for the purpose of pointing out that no warning that an unlawful and inhumane act will be committed can possibly be accepted as an excuse or palliation for that act or as an abatement of the responsibility for its commission.

Long acquainted as this government has been with the character of the Imperial German government and with the high principles of equity by which they have in the past been actuated and guided, the government of the United States cannot believe that the commanders of the vessels which committed these acts of lawlessness did so except under a misapprehension of the orders issued by the Imperial German naval authorities. It takes it for granted that, at least within the practical possibilities of every such case, the commanders even of submarines were expected to do nothing that would involve the lives of noncombatants or the safety of neutral ships, even at the cost of failing of their object of capture or destruction. It confidently expects, therefore, that the Imperial German government will disavow the acts of which the government of the United States complains, that they will make reparation so far as reparation is possible for injuries which are without measure, and that they will take immediate steps to prevent the recurrence of anything so obviously subversive of the principles of warfare for which the Imperial German government have in the past so wisely and so firmly contended.

The government and the people of the United States look to the Imperial German government for just, prompt, and enlightened action in this vital matter with the greater confidence because the United States and Germany are bound together, not only by special ties of friendship but also by the explicit stipulations of the treaty of 1828 between the United States and the Kingdom of Prussia.

Expressions of regret and offers of reparation in the case of the destruction of neutral ships sunk by mistake, while they may satisfy international obligations, if no loss of life results, cannot justify or excuse a practice, the natural and necessary effect of which is to subject neutral nations and neutral persons to new and immeasurable risks.

The Imperial German government will not expect the government of the United States to omit any word or any act necessary to the performance of its sacred duty of maintaining the rights of the United States and its citizens and of safeguarding their free exercise and enjoyment.

LEONARD WOOD: MILITARY UNPREPAREDNESS (1915)

Source: *The Military Obligation of Citizenship*, Princeton, 1915, Ch. 1: "The Policy of the United States in Raising and Maintaining Armies."

The people of the United States are singularly lacking in information concerning both the military history of their country and its military policy. Students in school and college as a rule receive entirely erroneous ideas on both of these subjects. The average young man, unless he has really made a study of the country's history, is firmly convinced that the Revolutionary War was characterized throughout by the highest quality of patriotism and devotion to the best interests of the country on the part of the people as a whole.

He is not at all familiar with the desperate struggle which was made by Washington, various colonial assemblies, and the Confederation of Colonies to keep in the field even a small force of troops. He hears very little of the bickerings, mutinies, desertions, and frequent changes of personnel which made the war a difficult one to conduct and served to bring out into strong relief the remarkable qualities of Washington—those qualities of patience, good judgment, discretion, and again patience, and more patience, which made it possible for him to hold the illy-equipped, disjointed, and discordant elements together, and to have always available some kind of a fighting force, although seldom an effective one.

We have as a nation neglected the lessons of past wars and have learned little from the example of the great military nations, and, as Emory Upton truthfully says: "Our general policy has followed closely that of China." Perhaps this statement may be somewhat extreme in all which applies to conditions up to the end of the Civil War, but it is not in any way extreme when applied to conditions which exist today. The great nations with policies to uphold and interests to defend have made what they believe to be adequate military preparation.

The United States has been drifting for years. No real military preparations of an adequate character have been made. Military preparedness means the organization of all the resources of a nation—men, material, and money—so that the full power of the nation may be promptly applied and continued at maximum strength for a considerable period of time. War today, when initiated by a country prepared for war, comes with great suddenness, because all preparations have been made in advance; plans have been worked out to the last detail, organization completed, and reserve supplies purchased and assembled long in advance, and the whole force of the mighty machine can be applied in a very brief period of time at any designated point.

Back of the machine itself is the railroad service, so organized as to be turned over immediately to the military authorities. Back of this come the civil hospitals, the bakeries, and the supply departments of all sorts, each with its responsibility fixed in case of operations within its area or in case of a demand for supplies in other sections of the theater of war. The capacity of every ship is known and plans completed for her use as a troop ship; and when war threatens, the whereabouts of the shipping is closely watched, and ships are assembled quietly to meet any demand which may be required for oversea operations. These are but an outline of what is meant by military preparedness.

Mere numbers of men and undeveloped military resources are of little value. It has been well said that in the sudden onrush of modern war undeveloped military resources are of no more use than an undeveloped gold mine in Alaska would be in a panic on Wall Street. The comparison is not overdrawn. You must remember, all of you, that this country has never yet engaged in war with a first-class power prepared for war.

You must remember also that once sea power is lost or held in check an enormous force can be landed on these shores within a month—a force sufficient to go where it will and to hold whatever it desires to hold.

Why have we failed to make adequate preparation? Partly because of ignorance of the true facts concerning our utter unpreparedness and partly due to a conceit fostered by the average Fourth of July orator and politician, through statements to the effect that we possess peculiar and remarkable military characteristics which make our soldiers trained and efficient without preparation,

and as good as equally brave and equally sound men of other countries who have spent years in training. Again there is the curious Anglo-Saxon prejudice against a large standing army and the feeling that it is always a menace to civil liberty.

In our past wars we were not confronted by great nations with highly organized military machines; steam navigation had not appeared; our possible enemies were without standing armies of any size and lacked entirely that complete military organization which characterizes them today. It took a long time to get troops together and prepare supplies for them and a considerable period of time to cross the ocean.

Our forefathers had more time to prepare. Then, again, they were more familiar with the use of arms; weapons were of a simple type; they could be made quickly and instruction in their use was a relatively simple matter.

Now, highly organized military establishments are the rule among our possible antagonists. Rapid steam transportation in vast amount is available. The arms of war are extremely complicated and costly; it takes a long time to make them and a long time to instruct soldiers in their use. In other words, today everything is in favor of the prepared aggressor and everything against the unready pacific nation. The blow comes more quickly and with greater force, and it is not possible to provide even a semblance of protection against it unless wise measures have been taken long in advance.

Since the foundation of the republic, war has existed as follows: Revolutionary War, 7 years; War of 1812–14, 2½ years; Mexican War, 2 years; Florida War, 7 years; Civil War, 4 years; War with Spain and Philippine Rebellion, 2 years—not to mention numerous Indian wars and internal disturbances requiring the use of troops.

We have struggled through these wars and have emerged generally successfully, but in none of them has there been any evidence of well-thought-out preparations or the application of a sound military policy. Our people remember only the success and forget entirely the great and unnecessary cost in blood and treasure in which our defective method of conducting these wars resulted. By faulty methods I mean that we have generally conducted war as a confederacy instead of as a nation. We have permitted altogether too much interference by states. Too many officers have been appointed by the governors of states. New regiments have been raised oftentimes in order that new officers might be appointed and political patronage increased, whereas the old regiments should have been filled up as they had acquired experience, some traditions and esprit, and were much more valuable than new regiments. This is seen in the Civil War in case of the Wisconsin organizations. Wisconsin had the good sense to veteranize her regiments, and the result is seen when one remembers the term "Iron Brigade" applied to a Wisconsin brigade.

Then again we have had frequently the intervention of civilians, either through the activities of the secretary of war or of the civil arms of the government. There has been a general lack of a sense of individual responsibility for military service. Reliance on volunteer enlistments has continued and has been one of the gravest sources of danger to the Republic. The experience of the Revolution should have taught us that it is not safe in a real war to depend upon volunteers. There is an enthusiastic response by a certain proportion of the best element in the early days of war, but this response cannot be counted upon to continue throughout a long war involving severe strains upon the population, nor is it right or just to throw the burden of military service upon a portion of the population. It is a universal obligation and the country will never be secure or safe until it is recognized as such and measures are taken to develop military preparation on a basis of universal military obligation....

The voluntary system failed us in the past and will fail us in the future. It is uncertain in operation, prevents organized preparation, tends to destroy that individual sense of obligation for military service which should be found in every citizen, costs excessively in life and treasure, and does not permit that condition of preparedness which must exist if we are to wage war successfully with any great power prepared for war.

The question is: What shall we do to adequately prepare ourselves for war without establishing a huge standing army or bringing about a condition which might be described as one of militarism, which term, as I use it, means the condition under which the military forces of a nation demand and secure special recognition, both socially and officially, and exercise an undue influence in the conduct of the civil affairs of the government, both at home and abroad? In other words, a condition which may be described as one under which the military element dominates the nation's policy. Nothing could be more unfortunate than the establishment of such a condition in this country or elsewhere, so far as development on normal lines is concerned. However, a condition of thorough preparedness can be established without creating a condition of militarism....

Do not place any dependence upon the statements of these charlatans who speak of a million men flocking to arms between sun and sun, but remember when you hear fallacies of this sort the words of old "Light-Horse Harry" Lee, which are as true today as they were when they were uttered. We must preserve our ideals, strive for world peace, and do what we can to build up the adjustment of international difficulties through arbitration, but we must not fail to give due heed to the conditions under which we live. Whatever we may hope for in the way of universal peace does not justify us in disregarding the conditions which surround us today.

If we want to hand down to our children the heritage which has come to us from our fathers, we must not place confidence in idle boasting but give serious heed to well-thought-out preparation and adopt a policy for the future with reference to our military establishment very different from that which has existed in the past. We can do this without violating our ideals. If I were to state such a military policy I would say, briefly, have an army sufficient for the peace needs of the nation, a good militia, an adequate navy, and behind them the largest possible number of men trained to be efficient soldiers if needed; but in time of peace following their ordinary civil occupations—ready to come when wanted. A country so prepared will have the largest possible measure of peace.

SUSAN B. ANTHONY: "THE STATUS OF WOMAN, PAST, PRESENT, AND FUTURE" (1897)

Source: *Arena*, May 1897.

Fifty years ago woman in the United States was without a recognized individuality in any department of life. No provision was made in public or private schools for her education in anything beyond the rudimentary branches. An educated woman was a rarity and was gazed upon with something akin to awe. The women who were known in the world of letters, in the entire country, could be easily counted upon the ten fingers. Margaret Fuller, educated by her father, a Harvard graduate and distinguished lawyer, stood preeminently at the head and challenged the admiration of such men as Emerson, Channing, and Greeley....

Such was the helpless, dependent, fettered condition of woman when the first Woman's Rights Convention was called just forty-nine years ago, at Seneca Falls, N.Y., by Elizabeth Cady Stanton and Lucretia Mott....

While there had been individual demands, from time to time, the first organized body to formulate a declaration of the rights of women was the one which met at Seneca Falls, July 19–20, 1848, and adjourned to meet at Rochester two weeks later. In the Declaration of Sentiments and the Resolutions there framed, every point was covered that, down to the present day, has been contended for by the advocates of equal rights for women. Every inequality of the existing laws and customs was carefully considered and a thorough and complete readjustment demanded....

Now, at the end of half a century, we find that, with few exceptions, all of the demands formulated at this convention have been granted. The great exception is the yielding of political rights, and toward this one point are directed now all the batteries of scorn, of ridicule, of denunciation that formerly poured their fire all along the line. Although not one of the predicted calamities occurred upon the granting of the other demands, the world is asked to believe that all of them will happen if this last stronghold is surrendered.

There is not space to follow the history of the last fifty years and study the methods by which these victories have been gained, but there is not one foot of advanced ground upon which women stand today that has not been obtained through the hard-fought battles of other women. The close of this 19th century finds every trade, vocation, and profession open to women, and every opportunity at their command for preparing themselves to follow these occupations.

The girls as well as the boys of a family now fit themselves for such careers as their tastes and abilities permit. A vast amount of the household drudgery that once monopolized the whole time and strength of the mother and daughters has been taken outside and turned over to machinery in vast establishments. A money value is placed upon the labor of women. The ban of social ostracism has been largely removed from the woman wage earner. She who can make for herself a place of distinction in any line of work receives commendation instead of condemnation. Woman is no longer compelled to marry for support, but may herself make her own home and earn her own financial independence.

With but few exceptions, the highest institutions of learning in the land are as freely opened to girls as to boys, and they may receive their degrees at legal, medical, and theological colleges, and practise their professions without hindrance. In the world of literature and art, women divide the honors with men; and our civil service rules have secured for them many thousands of remunerative positions under the government.

It is especially worthy of note that along with this general advancement of women has come a marked improvement in household methods. Woman's increased intelligence manifests itself in this department as conspicuously as in any other. Education, culture, mental discipline, business training develop far more capable mothers and housewives than were possible under the old regime. Men of the present generation give especial thought to comradeship in the selection of a wife, and she is no less desirable in their eyes because she is a college graduate or has learned the value and the management of money through having earned it.

There has been a radical revolution in the legal status of woman. In most states the old common law has been annulled by legislative enactment, through which partial justice, at least, has been done to married women. In nearly every state they may retain and control property owned at marriage and all they may receive by gift or inheritance thereafter, and also their earnings outside the home. They may sue and be sued, testify in the courts, and carry on business in their own name, but in no state have wives any ownership in the joint earnings.

In six or seven states, mothers have equal guardianship of the children. While in most states the divorce laws are the same for men and women, they never can bear equally upon both while all the property earned during marriage belongs wholly to the husband. There has been such a modification in public sentiment, however, that, in most cases, courts and juries show a marked leniency toward women.

The department of politics has been slowest to give admission to women. Suffrage is the pivotal right, and if it could have been secured at the beginning, women would not have been half a century in gaining the privileges enumerated above, for privileges they must be called so long as others may either give or take them away. If women could make the laws or elect those who make them, they would be in the position of sovereigns instead of subjects. Were they the political peers of man, they could command instead of having to beg, petition, and pray. Can it be possible it is for this reason that men have been so determined in their opposition to grant to women political power?

But even this stronghold is beginning to yield to the long and steady pressure. In twenty-five states women possess suffrage in school matters; in four states they have a limited suffrage in local affairs; in one state they have municipal suffrage; in four states they have full suffrage, local, state, and national. Women are becoming more and more interested in political questions and public affairs. Every campaign sees greater numbers in attendance at the meetings, and able woman speakers are now found upon the platforms of all parties. Especial efforts are made by politicians to obtain the support of women, and during the last campaign one of the presidential candidates held special meetings for women in the large cities throughout the country.

Some of the finest political writing in the great newspapers of the day is done by women, and the papers are extensively read by women of all classes. In many of the large cities women have formed civic clubs and are exercising a distinctive influence in municipal matters. In most of the states of the Union women are eligible for many offices, state and county superintendents, registers of deeds, etc. They are deputies to state, county, and city officials, notaries public, state librarians, and enrolling and engrossing clerks in the legislatures.

It follows, as a natural result, that in the states where women vote they are eligible to all offices. They have been sent as delegates to national conventions, made presidential electors, and are sitting today as members in both the upper and lower houses of the legislatures. In some towns all the offices are filled by women. These radical changes have been effected without any social upheaval or domestic earthquakes, family relations have suffered no disastrous changes, and the men of the states where women vote furnish the strongest testimony in favor of woman suffrage.

There is no more striking illustration of the progress that has been made by woman than that afforded by her changed position in the church. Under the old regime the Quakers were the only sect who recognized the equality of women. Other denominations enforced the command of St. Paul, that women should keep silence in the churches. A few allowed the women to lift up their voices in class and prayer meetings, but they had no vote in matters of church government. Even the missionary and charity work was in the hands of men.

Now the Unitarians, Universalists, Congregationalists, Wesleyan and Protestant Methodists, Christians, Free-Will Baptists, and possibly a few others, ordain women as ministers, and many parishes, in all parts of the country, are presided over by women preachers. The charitable and missionary work of the churches is practically turned over to women, who raise and disburse immense sums of money. While many of the great denominations still refuse to ordain women, to allow them a seat in their councils, or a vote in matters of church government, yet women themselves are, in a large measure, responsible for this state of affairs.

Forming, as they do, from two-thirds to three-fourths of the membership, raising the greater part of the funds, and carrying on the active work of the church, when they unite their forces and assert their rights, the small minority of men, who have usurped the authority, will be obliged to yield to their just demands. The creeds of the churches will recognize woman's equality before God as the codes of the states have acknowledged it before man and the law.

By far the larger part of the progressive movements just enumerated have taken place during the last twenty-five years, and the progress has been most rapid during the last half of this quarter of a century. With the advantages already obtained, with the great liberalizing of public sentiment, and with the actual proof that the results of enlarged opportunities for women have been for the betterment of society, the next decade ought to see the completion of the struggle for the equality of the sexes.

The hardest of the battles have been fought, and, while there is still need for both generals and soldiers, the greatest necessity is for the body of women to take possession and hold the ground that has been gained. It is not sufficient that women should fill positions as well as men; they must give vastly better satisfaction in order to prove their claims. There is an urgent demand for women of the highest character and intelligence, because the whole sex will be judged by the few who come forward to assume these new duties.

While by the momentum already gained the reforms demanded would eventually come, women have learned the value of organization and united, systematic work in securing the best and speediest results. It is no longer necessary to make an effort for further educational facilities. The few universities which still close their doors to women will ultimately be compelled to open them by the exigencies of the situation. There are no longer any fences around the industrial field, although men will continue to have the best pickings in the pasture so long as women are disfranchised. There will

be a gradual yielding of the laws in recognition of woman's improved position in all departments, but here also there never will be complete equality until women themselves help to make laws and elect lawmakers. In view of this indisputable fact, the advanced thinkers are agreed that the strongest efforts should be concentrated upon this point.

From that little convention at Seneca Falls, with a following of a handful of women scattered through half-a-dozen different states, we have now the great National Association, with headquarters in New York City, and auxiliaries in almost every state in the Union. These state bodies are effecting a thorough system of county and local organizations for the purpose of securing legislation favorable to women, and especially to obtain amendments to their state constitutions. As evidence of the progress of public opinion, more than half of the legislatures in session during the past winter have discussed and voted upon bills for the enfranchisement of women, and in most of them they were adopted by one branch and lost by a very small majority in the other. The legislatures of Washington and South Dakota have submitted woman-suffrage amendments to their electors for 1898, and vigorous campaigns will be made in those states during the next two years.

For a quarter of a century Wyoming has stood as a conspicuous object lesson in woman suffrage, and is now reinforced by the three neighboring states of Colorado, Utah, and Idaho. With this central group, standing on the very crest of the Rocky Mountains, the spirit of justice and freedom for women cannot fail to descend upon all the Western and Northwestern states. No one who makes a careful study of this question can help but believe that, in a very few years, all the states west of the Mississippi River will have enfranchised their women.

While the efforts of each state are concentrated upon its own legislature, all of the states combined in the national organization are directing their energies toward securing a Sixteenth Amendment to the Constitution of the United States. The demands of this body have been received with respectful and encouraging attention from Congress. Hearings have been granted by the committees of both houses, resulting, in a number of instances, in favorable reports. Upon one occasion the question was brought to a discussion in the Senate and received the affirmative vote of one-third of the members.

Until woman has obtained "that right protective of all other rights—the ballot," this agitation must still go on, absorbing the time and the energy of our best and strongest women. Who can measure the advantages that would result if the magnificent abilities of these women could be devoted to the needs of government, society, home, instead of being consumed in the struggle to obtain their birthright of individual freedom? Until this be gained we can never know, we cannot even prophesy, the capacity and power of woman for the uplifting of humanity.

It may be delayed longer than we think; it may be here sooner than we expect; but the day will come when man will recognize woman as his peer, not only at the fireside but in the councils of the nation. Then, and not until then, will there be the perfect comradeship, the ideal union between the sexes that shall result in the highest development of the race. What this shall be we may not attempt to define, but this we know, that only good can come to the individual or to the nation through the rendering of exact justice.

CHARLES A. BEARD: REASONS FOR HIS RESIGNATION FROM COLUMBIA UNIVERSITY (1917)

Source: *The New Republic*, Dec. 29, 1917.

It has been insinuated by certain authorities of Columbia University that I resigned in a fit of unjustified petulance, and I therefore beg to submit the following statement:

1. My first real experience with the inner administration of the university came with the retirement of Prof. John W. Burgess. For some time before his withdrawal, his work in American constitutional law had been carried by Professor X and it was the desire of the members of the faculty that the latter should be appointed Ruggles Professor to succeed Mr. Burgess. But Mr. X had published a book in which he justified criticism of the Supreme Court as a means of bringing

our constitutional law into harmony with our changing social and economic life. He was therefore excluded from the Ruggles professorship. It was given to Mr. W. D. Guthrie, a successful corporation lawyer, and a partner of one of the trustees of the university.

It was understood that Mr. Guthrie should give one lecture a week for one semester each year in return for the high honor. Mr. Butler is constantly saying that all matters relating to appointment, fitness, and tenure are left to the appropriate faculties, or words to this effect. As a matter of plain fact, the Faculty of Political Science as such was not consulted in advance in the selection of the Ruggles Professor. The whole affair was settled by backstairs negotiation, and it was understood by all of us who had any part in the business that no person with progressive or liberal views would be acceptable.

Mr. Guthrie was duly appointed. Of his contributions to learning I shall not speak, but I can say that he did not attend faculty meetings, help in conducting doctors' examinations, or assume the burdens imposed upon other professors. This was the way in which the first important vacancy in the Faculty of Political Science was filled after my connection with the institution.

2. My second experience with the administration of the university came in 1916. On April 21 of that year I delivered an address before the National Conference of Community Centers in which I advocated the use of the schools as the centers for the discussion of public questions. A few weeks before, a speaker at one of the school forums was alleged to have said, "To hell with the flag," and for that reason a number of persons had urged the closing of school centers altogether. Indeed, some of the speakers at the above-mentioned conference advocated a sort of censorship for all school forums.

In my address I merely took the reasonable and moderate view that the intemperance of one man should not drive us into closing the schools to others. The reports in the newspapers, with one exception, were fairly accurate. But one sensational sheet accused me of approving the sentiment, "To hell with the flag." Dr. Butler, who had had large experience with frenzied journalism, quite rightly took the view that I had been the victim of the headline writer and advised me to do my best to correct the wrong impression and then forget it. I immediately wrote to all of the papers and sought to remove the misunderstanding that had arisen.

Nevertheless, I was summoned before the Committee on Education of the Board of Trustees. I complied because I wanted to clear up any wrong impressions which the members entertained concerning the nature of my address before the Community Center Conference.

As soon as the committee of the trustees opened the inquiry, I speedily disposed of the "flag incident" by showing that I had said nothing that could be construed as endorsing in any way the objectionable language in question. No one doubted my word. Indeed, I had available abundant testimony from reliable men and women who had heard the address. The record was thus soon set straight.

The inquiry as to the flag incident being at an end I prepared to leave the room when I was utterly astonished to have Mr. Bangs and Mr. Coudert launch into an inquisition into my views and teachings. For half an hour I was "grilled" by these gentlemen. Dr. Butler and certain colleagues from the Faculty of Political Science (who were present at the inquisition) made no attempt to stop the proceedings. Mr. Coudert, who had once privately commended my book on the Constitution as "admirably well done," and opening up "a most fertile field," denounced my teachings in vigorous language, in which he was strongly seconded by Mr. Bangs.

I realize now that I should have refused to remain in the room, but I was taken unaware and stunned by the procedure. When the inquisitors satisfied themselves, the chairman of the committee ordered me to warn all other men in my department against teachings "likely to inculcate disrespect for American institutions." I repeated my order to my colleagues, who received it with a shout of derision, one of them asking me whether Tammany Hall and the pork barrel were not American institutions!

I reported to my colleagues in the Faculty of Political Science that I had

been subjected by the committee of the trustees to a "general doctrinal inquisition," and urged them, at an informal meeting, to establish a rule that a professor should be examined in matters of opinion only by his peers, namely, men of standing in his profession. Several caucuses of the faculty were held and it was generally agreed that the proceedings of the trustees were highly reprehensible. Action doubtless should have been taken by the faculty at the time if we had not been told by Dean Woodbridge that "the trustees had learned their lesson and that such an inquisition would never happen again."

We were also informed that some of the trustees were "after" President Butler for his pacifist writings and affiliations, and that if the faculty took a firm stand in matters of doctrinal inquisition an open conflict might ensue. In a long conversation President Butler urged me to drop the whole "miserable business" and go on about my work. For the sake of "peace" I consented.

I should not forget, however, the cases of Professor Kendrick and Dr. Fraser, who had been haled before the committee of the trustees on the trivial charge that they had criticized Plattsburg and military discipline at a student meeting some time early in 1916. Their cases I regarded as peculiarly open to objection because they were not even accused of saying anything that was indecent or vulgar or unpatriotic. Nevertheless, I dropped the whole matter on the assurance that such an inquisition would not happen again and that the trustees "had learned their lesson."

3. Though I did not agree with some of my exuberant colleagues that a "great battle for academic freedom had been won," I was ready to abide by their decision. Then, to our utter astonishment, the trustees at their March meeting in 1917 gave to the press a set of resolutions instructing a committee "to inquire and ascertain" whether certain doctrines were being taught in the university. President Butler, in whose name we had been assured that no such inquisition would ever happen again, avoided the issue by taking a vacation and leaving the faculties to deal with the situation.

The action of the Faculty of Political Science was prompt. An informal meeting was held at which a resolution in the following tenor was unanimously adopted:

Whereas the resolution of the trustees by its very terms implies a general doctrinal inquisition, insults the members of the faculty by questioning their loyalty to their country, violates every principle of academic freedom, and betrays a profound misconception of the true function of the university in the advancement of learning, Be it resolved that we will not individually or collectively lend any countenance to such an inquiry.

The trustees were forced to abandon their plan for a general inquisition. Indeed, when they learned of the spirit of the Faculty of Political Science and other faculties, they hastily disclaimed any intention of making a "doctrinal inquiry"—as their resolution of March 1917 clearly implied.

It was agreed that such matters should be handled in cooperation with a committee of nine representing the faculties.

4. Notwithstanding this promise of cooperation on the part of the trustees and the committee of nine representing the teaching force, the trustees ignored the recommendations of that committee in the cases of Professors Dana and Cattell and dismissed these gentlemen summarily in the autumn of 1917, after wrongfully charging them with treason and sedition. Prof. John Dewey resigned from the committee of nine, and the body which was to safeguard the interests of the professors collapsed in ignominy.

5. Some time before Professors Cattell and Dana were expelled, another professor was summarily thrown out of the university without warning or trial. No reasons for his expulsion were advanced, and a polite inquiry addressed by his colleagues to President Butler asking for information remained unanswered.

6. Dr. Leon Fraser was an instructor in politics in Columbia College. With this office he combined that of assistant to Dean Keppel and Dr. Butler in the Association for International Conciliation. Dr. Fraser was assigned the task of organizing forces in colleges throughout the country on pacifism and international conciliation. In other words, he was paid by these gentlemen to engage

in pacifist propaganda. In a moment of youthful enthusiasm, early in 1916, Dr. Fraser made some critical remark about the military camp at Plattsburg. For this he was haled before a committee of the trustees.

A year later, namely in the spring of 1917, my department was warned not to renominate Dr. Fraser for reappointment because he was not acceptable to Mr. Bangs, one of the trustees. In spite of our orders we did renominate Dr. Fraser, but before action could be taken by the trustees, he, along with other instructors, was dropped on the assumption that the war would reduce materially the number of students in the college. But not content with dropping him, Mr. Butler informed the college authorities that in case the attendance in the college in the autumn warranted the appointment of additional instructors, under no circumstances should Dr. Fraser be renominated.

In truth, therefore, if not in theory, Dr. Fraser was expelled from the college without notice or hearing. In view of the fact that Mr. Fraser had been inspired by Mr. Butler and Mr. Keppel to engage in pacifist propaganda and had been paid by them for doing it, it seemed to me that they should at least have demanded and insisted upon having a full and fair hearing of the charges against their youthful adherent, especially as those charges grew out of his "pacifist teachings."

7. We are informed by Dr. Butler that nominations for appointment and promotions come from the faculties. Such may be the theory but it is the practice for the trustees and president to warn the committee in charge of appointments and promotions against recommending "unacceptable" persons. For example, when the committee on instruction of the Faculty of Political Science, of which I was a member, was considering promotions last spring, it was informed at the outset by "the committee of one on rumor from the president's office" that "certain of the trustees" would not approve the promotion of Professor Y because he had used "disrespectful language" in speaking of the Supreme Court. Professor Y was not recommended for promotion and the trustees could proudly say that they had not rejected a faculty recommendation!

Mr. Butler cannot conceive of a scholar's entertaining progressive ideas. Once, in asking me to recommend an instructor to a neighboring college, he distinctly pointed out that a man of "Bull Moose" proclivities would not be acceptable.

8. Early in October 1917, I was positively and clearly informed by two responsible officers of the university that another doctrinal inquisition was definitely scheduled for an early date. It was the evident purpose of a small group of the trustees (unhindered, if not aided, by Mr. Butler) to take advantage of the state of war to drive out or humiliate or terrorize every man who held progressive, liberal, or unconventional views on political matters in no way connected with the war. The institution was to be reduced below the level of a department store or factory, and I therefore tendered my resignation.

I make no claims in behalf of academic freedom, though I think they are worthy of consideration: I have merely held that teachers should not be expelled without a full and fair hearing by their peers, surrounded by all of the safeguards of judicial process. Professors in Columbia University have been subjected to humiliating doctrinal inquisitions by the trustees, they have been expelled without notice or hearing, and their appointment and promotion depend upon securing, in advance, the favor of certain trustees. Without that favor, scholarship and learning avail nothing.

These facts I submit to the candid and impartial reader. I believe that they constitute a full and unanswerable indictment of the prevailing method at Columbia University under the administration of Dr. Nicholas Murray Butler.

WOODROW WILSON: PEACE WITHOUT VICTORY (1917)

Source: 64 Congress, 2 Session, Senate Document No. 685: "A League for Peace."

On the 18th of December last, I addressed an identic note to the governments of the nations now at war requesting them to state, more definitely than they had yet been stated by either group of belligerents, the terms upon which they would deem it possible to make peace. I spoke on behalf of humanity and of the rights of all neutral nations like our own, many of whose most vital interests the war puts in constant jeopardy.

The Central Powers united in a reply which stated merely that they were ready to meet their antagonists in conference to discuss terms of peace. The Entente Powers have replied much more definitely and have stated, in general terms, indeed, but with sufficient definiteness to imply details, the arrangements, guarantees, and acts of reparation which they deem to be the indispensable conditions of a satisfactory settlement. We are that much nearer a definite discussion of the peace which shall end the present war. We are that much nearer the discussion of the international concert which must thereafter hold the world at peace.

In every discussion of the peace that must end this war, it is taken for granted that that peace must be followed by some definite concert of power which will make it virtually impossible that any such catastrophe should ever overwhelm us again. Every lover of mankind, every sane and thoughtful man must take that for granted.

I have sought this opportunity to address you because I thought that I owed it to you, as the council associated with me in the final determination of our international obligations, to disclose to you without reserve the thought and purpose that have been taking form in my mind in regard to the duty of our government in the days to come, when it will be necessary to lay afresh and upon a new plan the foundations of peace among the nations.

It is inconceivable that the people of the United States should play no part in that great enterprise. To take part in such a service will be the opportunity for which they have sought to prepare themselves by the very principles and purposes of their polity and the approved practices of their government ever since the days when they set up a new nation in the high and honorable hope that it might, in all that it was and did, show mankind the way to liberty.

They cannot in honor withhold the service to which they are now about to be challenged. They do not wish to withhold it. But they owe it to themselves and to the other nations of the world to state the conditions under which they will feel free to render it.

That service is nothing less than this, to add their authority and their power to the authority and force of other nations to guarantee peace and justice throughout the world. Such a settlement cannot now be long postponed. It is right that before it comes, this government should frankly formulate the conditions upon which it would feel justified in asking our people to approve its formal and solemn adherence to a League for Peace. I am here to attempt to state those conditions.

The present war must first be ended; but we owe it to candor and to a just regard for the opinion of mankind to say that, so far as our participation in guarantees of future peace is concerned, it makes a great deal of difference in what way and upon what terms it is ended. The treaties and agreements which bring it to an end must embody terms which will create a peace that is worth guaranteeing and preserving, a peace that will win the approval of mankind, not merely a peace that will serve the several interests and immediate aims of the nations engaged. We shall have no voice in determining what those terms shall be, but we shall, I feel sure, have a voice in determining whether they shall be made lasting or not by the guarantes of a universal covenant; and our judgment upon what is fundamental and essential as a condition precedent to permanency should be spoken now, not afterwards when it may be too late.

No covenant of cooperative peace that does not include the peoples of the New World can suffice to keep the future safe against war; and yet there is only one sort of peace that the peoples of America could join in guaranteeing. The elements of that peace must be elements that engage the confidence and satisfy the principles of the American governments, elements consistent with their political faith and with the practical convictions which the peoples of America have once for all embraced and undertaken to defend.

I do not mean to say that any American government would throw any obstacle in the way of any terms of peace the governments now at war might agree upon or seek to upset them when made, whatever they might be. I only take it for granted that mere terms of peace between the belligerents will not satisfy even the belligerents themselves. Mere agreements may not make peace secure. It will be absolutely necessary that a force be created as a guarantor of the permanency of the settlement so much greater than the force of any nation now engaged, or any alliance hitherto formed or projected, that no nation, no probable combination of nations, could face or withstand it. If the peace presently to be made is to endure, it must be a peace made secure by the organized major force of mankind.

The terms of the immediate peace agreed upon will determine whether it is a peace for which such a guarantee can be secured. The question upon which the whole future peace and policy of the world depends is this: Is the present war a struggle for a just and secure peace, or only for a new balance of power? If it be only a struggle for a new balance of power, who will guarantee, who can guarantee the stable equilibrium of the new arrangement? Only a tranquil Europe can be a stable Europe. There must be, not a balance of power but a community of power; not organized rivalries but an organized, common peace.

Fortunately we have received very explicit assurances on this point. The statesmen of both of the groups of nations now arrayed against one another have said, in terms that could not be misinterpreted, that it was no part of the purpose they had in mind to crush their antagonists. But the implications of these assurances may not be equally clear to all—may not be the same on both sides of the water. I think it will be serviceable if I attempt to set forth what we understand them to be.

They imply, first of all, that it must be a peace without victory. It is not pleasant to say this. I beg that I may be permitted to put my own interpretation upon it and that it may be understood that no other interpretation was in my thought. I am seeking only to face realities and to face them without soft concealments. Victory would mean peace forced upon the loser, a victor's terms imposed upon the vanquished. It would be accepted in humiliation, under duress, at an intolerable sacrifice, and would leave a sting, a resentment, a bitter memory upon which terms of peace would rest, not permanently but only as upon quicksand. Only a peace between equals can last. Only a peace the very principle of which is equality and a common participation in a common benefit. The right state of mind, the right feeling between nations, is as necessary for a lasting peace as is the just settlement of vexed questions of territory or of racial and national allegiance.

The equality of nations upon which peace must be founded if it is to last must be an equality of rights; the guarantees exchanged must neither recognize nor imply a difference between big nations and small, between those that are powerful and those that are weak. Right must be based upon the common strength, not upon the individual strength, of the nations upon whose concert peace will depend. Equality of territory or of resources there of course cannot be; nor any other sort of equality not gained in the ordinary peaceful and legitimate development of the peoples themselves.

But no one asks or expects anything more than an equality of rights. Mankind is looking now for freedom of life, not for equipoises of power.

And there is a deeper thing involved than even equality of right among organized nations. No peace can last, or ought to last, which does not recognize and accept the principle that governments derive all their just powers from the consent of the governed, and that no right anywhere exists to hand peoples about from sovereignty to sovereignty as if they were property. I take it for granted, for instance, if I may venture upon a single example, that statesmen everywhere are agreed that there should be a united, independent, and autonomous Poland, and that, henceforth, inviolable security of life, of worship, and of industrial and social development should be guaranteed to all peoples who have lived hitherto under the power of governments devoted to a faith and purpose hostile to their own.

I speak of this, not because of any desire to exalt an abstract political principle which has always been held very dear by those who have sought to build up liberty in America but for the same reason that I have spoken of the other conditions of peace which seem to me clearly indispensable—because I wish frankly to uncover realities. Any peace which does not recognize and accept this principle will inevitably be upset. It will not rest upon the affections or the convictions of mankind. The ferment of spirit of whole populations will fight subtly and

constantly against it, and all the world will sympathize. The world can be at peace only if its life is stable, and there can be no stability where the will is in rebellion, where there is not tranquillity of spirit and a sense of justice, of freedom, and of right.

So far as practicable, moreover, every great people now struggling toward a full development of its resources and of its powers should be assured a direct outlet to the great highways of the sea. Where this cannot be done by the cession of territory, it can no doubt be done by the neutralization of direct rights of way under the general guarantee which will assure the peace itself. With a right comity of arrangement, no nation need be shut away from free access to the open paths of the world's commerce.

And the paths of the sea must alike in law and in fact be free. The freedom of the seas is the sine qua non of peace, equality, and cooperation. No doubt a somewhat radical reconsideration of many of the rules of international practice hitherto thought to be established may be necessary in order to make the seas indeed free and common in practically all circumstances for the use of mankind, but the motive for such changes is convincing and compelling. There can be no trust or intimacy between the peoples of the world without them. The free, constant, unthreatened intercourse of nations is an essential part of the process of peace and of development. It need not be difficult either to define or to secure the freedom of the seas if the governments of the world sincerely desire to come to an agreement concerning it.

It is a problem closely connected with the limitation of naval armaments and the cooperation of the navies of the world in keeping the seas at once free and safe. And the question of limiting naval armaments opens the wider and perhaps more difficult question of the limitation of armies and of all programs of military preparation. Difficult and delicate as these questions are, they must be faced with the utmost candor and decided in a spirit of real accommodation if peace is to come with healing in its wings, and come to stay.

Peace cannot be had without concession and sacrifice. There can be no sense of safety and equality among the nations if great preponderating armaments are henceforth to continue here and there to be built up and maintained. The statesmen of the world must plan for peace, and nations must adjust and accommodate their policy to it as they have planned for war and made ready for pitiless contest and rivalry. The question of armaments, whether on land or sea, is the most immediately and intensely practical question connected with the future fortunes of nations and of mankind.

I have spoken upon these great matters without reserve and with the utmost explicitness because it has seemed to me to be necessary if the world's yearning desire for peace was anywhere to find free voice and utterance. Perhaps I am the only person in high authority among all the peoples of the world who is at liberty to speak and hold nothing back. I am speaking as an individual, and yet I am speaking also, of course, as the responsible head of a great government, and I feel confident that I have said what the people of the United States would wish me to say.

May I not add that I hope and believe that I am in effect speaking for liberals and friends of humanity in every nation and of every program of liberty? I would fain believe that I am speaking for the silent mass of mankind everywhere who have as yet had no place or opportunity to speak their real hearts out concerning the death and ruin they see to have come already upon the persons and the homes they hold most dear.

And in holding out the expectation that the people and government of the United States will join the other civilized nations of the world in guaranteeing the permanence of peace upon such terms as I have named I speak with the greater boldness and confidence because it is clear to every man who can think that there is in this promise no breach in either our traditions or our policy as a nation, but a fulfillment, rather, of all that we have professed or striven for.

I am proposing, as it were, that the nations should with one accord adopt the doctrine of President Monroe as the doctrine of the world: that no nation should seek to extend its polity over any other nation or people, but that every people should be left free to determine its own polity, its own way of development—unhindered, unthreatened, unafraid, the little along with the great and powerful.

I am proposing that all nations henceforth avoid entangling alliances which would draw them into competitions of power, catch them in a net of intrigue and selfish rivalry, and disturb their own affairs with influences intruded from without. There is no entangling alliance in a concert of power. When all unite to act in the same sense and with the same purpose, all act in the common interest and are free to live their own lives under a common protection.

I am proposing government by the consent of the governed; that freedom of the seas which in international conference after conference representatives of the United States have urged with the eloquence of those who are the convinced disciples of liberty; and that moderation of armaments which makes of armies and navies a power for order merely, not an instrument of aggression or of selfish violence.

These are American principles, American policies. We could stand for no others. And they are also the principles and policies of forward-looking men and women everywhere, of every modern nation, of every enlightened community. They are the principles of mankind and must prevail.

WOODROW WILSON: FOURTEEN POINTS (1918)

Source: *Congressional Record*, Washington, 64 Cong., 2 Sess., pp. 680–681.

We entered this war because violations of right had occurred which touched us to the quick and made the life of our own people impossible unless they were corrected and the world secure once for all against their recurrence What we demand in this war, therefore, is nothing peculiar to ourselves. It is that the world be made fit and safe to live in; and particularly that it be made safe for every peaceloving nation which, like our own, wishes to live its own life, determine its own institutions, be assured of justice and fair dealing by the other peoples of the world as against force and selfish aggression. All the peoples of the world are in effect partners in this interest, and for our own part we see very clearly that unless justice be done to others it will not be done to us. The programme of the world's peace, therefore, is our programme; and that programme, the only possible programme, as we see it, is this:

1. Open covenants of peace, openly arrived at, after which there shall be no private international understandings of any kind but diplomacy shall proceed always frankly and in the public view.

2. Absolute freedom of navigation upon the seas, outside territorial waters, alike in peace and in war, except as the seas may be closed in whole or in part by international action for the enforcement of international covenants.

3. The removal, so far as possible, of all economic barriers and the establishment of an equality of trade conditions among all the nations consenting to the peace and associating themselves for its maintenance.

4. Adequate guarantees given and taken that national armaments will be reduced to the lowest point consistent with domestic safety.

5. A free, open-minded, and absolutely impartial adjustment of all colonial claims, based upon a strict observance of the principle that in determining all such questions of sovereignty the interests of the populations concerned must have equal weight with the equitable claims of the government whose title is to be determined.

6. The evacuation of all Russian territory and such a settlement of all questions affecting Russia as will secure the best and freest coöperation of the other nations of the world in obtaining for her an unhampered and unembarrassed opportunity for the independent determination of her own political development and national policy and assure her of a sincere welcome into the society of free nations under institutions of her own choosing; and, more than a welcome, assistance also of every kind that she may need and may herself desire. The treatment accorded Russia by her sister nations in the months to come will be the acid test of their good will, of their comprehension of her needs as distinguished from their own interests, and of their intelligent and unselfish sympathy.

7. Belgium, the whole world will agree, must be evacuated and restored, without any attempt to limit the sovereignty which she enjoys in common with all other free nations. No other single act will serve as this will serve to restore confidence among the nations in the laws which they have themselves set and determined for the government of their relations with one another. Without this healing act the whole structure and validity of international law is forever impaired.

8. All French territory should be freed and the invaded portions restored, and the wrong done to France by Prussia in 1871 in the matter of Alsace-Lorraine, which has unsettled the peace of the world for nearly fifty years, should be righted, in order that peace may once more be made secure in the interest of all.

9. A readjustment of the frontiers of Italy should be effected along clearly recognizable lines of nationality.

10. The peoples of Austria-Hungary, whose place among the nations we wish to see safeguarded and assured, should be accorded the freest opportunity of autonomous development.

11. Rumania, Serbia, and Montenegro should be evacuated; occupied territories restored; Serbia accorded free and secure access to the sea; and the relations of the several Balkan states to one another determined by friendly counsel along historically established lines of allegiance and nationality; and international guarantees of the political and economic independence and territorial integrity of the several Balkan states should be entered into.

12. The Turkish portions of the present Ottoman Empire should be assured a secure sovereignty, but the other nationalities which are now under Turkish rule should be assured an undoubted security

of life and an absolutely unmolested opportunity of autonomous development, and the Dardanelles should be permanently opened as a free passage to the ships and commerce of all nations under international guarantes.

13. An independent Polish state should be erected which should include the territories inhabited by indisputably Polish populations, which should be assured a free and secure access to the sea, and whose political and economic independence and territorial integrity should be guaranteed by international covenant.

14. A general association of nations must be formed under specific covenants for the purpose of affording mutual guarantees of political independence and territorial integrity to great and small states alike.

In regard to these essential rectifications of wrong and assertions of right we feel ourselves to be intimate partners of all the governments and peoples associated together against the Imperialists. We cannot be separated in interest or divided in purpose. We stand together until the end.

For such arrangements and covenants we are willing to fight and to continue to fight until they are achieved; but only because we wish the right to prevail and desire a just and stable peace such as can be secured only by removing the chief provocations to war, which this program does remove. We have no jealousy of German greatness, and there is nothing in this program that impairs it. We grudge her no achievement or distinction of learning or of pacific enterprise such as have made her record very bright and very enviable. We do not wish to injure her or to block in any way her legitimate influence or power. We do not wish to fight her either with arms or with hostile arrangements of trade if she is willing to associate herself with us and the other peace-loving nations of the world in covenants of justice and law and fair dealing. We wish her only to accept a place of equality among the peoples of the world,—the new world in which we now live,—instead of a place of mastery.

HENRY CABOT LODGE: RESERVATIONS WITH REGARD TO THE TREATY OF VERSAILLES (1919)

Source: *Congressional Record*, 66 Cong., 1 Sess., pp. 8777–8778; 8768–8769.

Resolved (two-thirds of the senators present concurring therein), that the Senate advise and consent to the ratification of the treaty of peace with Germany concluded at Versailles on the 28th day of June, 1919, subject to the following reservations and understandings, which are hereby made a part and condition of this resolution of ratification, which ratification is not to take effect or bind the United States until the said reservations and understandings adopted by the Senate have been accepted by an exchange of notes as a part and a condition of this resolution of ratification by at least three of the four principal allied and associated powers, to wit, Great Britain, France, Italy, and Japan:

- The United States so understands and construes Article 1 that in case of notice of withdrawal from the League of Nations, as provided in said article, the United States shall be the sole judge as to whether all its international obligations and all its obligations under the said Covenant have been fulfilled, and notice of withdrawal by the United States may be given by a concurrent resolution of the Congress of the United States.
- The United States assumes no obligation to preserve the territorial integrity or political independence of any other country or to interfere in controversies between nations—whether members of the League or not—under the provisions of Article 10, or to employ the military or naval forces of the United States under any article of the treaty for any purpose, unless in any particular case the Congress, which, under the Constitution, has the sole power to declare war or authorize the employment of the military or naval forces of the United States, shall by act or joint resolution so provide.
- No mandate shall be accepted by the United States under Article 22, Part 1, or any other provision of the treaty of peace with Germany, except by action of the Congress of the United States.

- The United States reserves to itself exclusively the right to decide what questions are within its domestic jurisdiction and declares that all domestic and political questions relating wholly or in part to its internal affairs, including immigration, labor, coastwise traffic, the tariff, commerce, the suppression of traffic in women and children, and in opium and other dangerous drugs, and all other domestic questions, are solely within the jurisdiction of the United States and are not under this treaty to be submitted in any way either to arbitration or to the consideration of the Council or of the Assembly of the League of Nations, or any agency thereof, or to the decision or recommendation of any other power.
- The United States will not submit to arbitration or to inquiry by the Assembly or by the Council of the League of Nations provided for in said treaty of peace any questions which in the judgment of the United States depend upon or relate to its long-established policy, commonly known as the Monroe Doctrine; said doctrine is to be interpreted by the United States alone and is hereby declared to be wholly outside the jurisdiction of said League of Nations and entirely unaffected by any provision contained in the said treaty of peace with Germany.

- The United States withholds its assent to Articles 156, 157, and 158, and reserves full liberty of action with respect to any controversy which may arise under said articles between the Republic of China and the Empire of Japan.
- The Congress of the United States will provide by law for the appointment of the representatives of the United States in the Assembly and the Council of the League of Nations, and may in its discretion provide for the participation of the United States in any commission, committee, tribunal, court, council, or conference, or in the selection of any members thereof, and for the appointment of members of said commissions, committees, tribunals, courts, councils, or conferences, or any other representatives under the treaty of peace, or in carrying out its provisions; and until such participation and appointment have been so provided for and the powers and duties of such representatives have been defined by law, no person shall represent the United States under either said League of Nations or the treaty of peace with Germany or be authorized to perform any act for or on behalf of the United States thereunder; and no citizen of the United States shall be selected or appointed as a member of said commissions, committees, tribunals, courts, councils, or conferences except with the approval of the Senate of the United States.
- The United States understands that the Reparation Commission will regulate or interfere with exports from the United States to Germany, or from Germany to the United States, only when the United States by act or joint resolution of Congress approves such regulation or interference.
- The United States shall not be obligated to contribute to any expenses of the League of Nations, or of the Secretariat, or of any commission, or committee, or conference, or other agency organized under the League of Nations or under the treaty or for the purpose of carrying out the treaty provisions, unless and until an appropriation of funds available for such expenses shall have been made by the Congress of the United States.
- If the United States shall at any time adopt any plan for the limitation of armaments proposed by the Council of the League of Nations under the provisions of Article 8, it reserves the right to increase such armaments without the consent of the Council whenever the United States is threatened with invasion or engaged in war.
- The United States reserves the right to permit, in its discretion,

the nationals of a Covenant-breaking state, as defined in Article 16 of the Covenant of the League of Nations, residing within the United States or in countries other than that violating said Article 16, to continue their commercial, financial, and personal relations with the nationals of the United States.

- Nothing in Articles 296, 297, or in any of the annexes thereto or in any other article, section, or annex of the treaty of peace with Germany shall, as against citizens of the United States, be taken to mean any confirmation, ratification, or approval of any act otherwise illegal or in contravention of the rights of citizens of the United States.

- The United States withholds its assent to Part XIII (Articles 387 to 427, inclusive) unless Congress by act or joint resolution shall hereafter make provision for representation in the organization established by said Part XIII; and in such event the participation of the United States will be governed and conditioned by the provisions of such act or joint resolution.

- The United States assumes no obligation to be bound by any election, decision, report, or finding of the Council or Assembly in which any member of the League and its self-governing dominions, colonies, or parts of empire, in the aggregate, have cast more than one vote, and assumes no obligation to be bound by any decision, report, or finding of the Council or Assembly arising out of any dispute between the United States and any member of the League if such member, or any self-governing dominion, colony, empire, or part of empire united with it politically has voted.

GLOSSARY

armistice Temporary suspension of hostilities by agreement between the opponents.

augur To give promise of.

bully pulpit A prominent public position (as a political office) that provides an opportunity for expounding one's views.

chauvinist One with excessive, especially blind, patriotism.

collectivism A political or economic theory advocating collective control, especially over production and distribution.

conscription Compulsory enrollment of persons, especially for military service.

dollar diplomacy Diplomacy that seeks to strengthen the power of a country or effect its purposes in foreign relations through the use of its financial resources.

exigency That which is required in a particular situation ; a state of affairs that makes urgent demands.

factitious Produced by humans rather than by natural forces.

flotilla A navy organizational unit consisting of two or more squadrons of small warships.

gentleman's agreement An agreement secured only by the honour of the participants.

hegemony Preponderant influence or authority.

identic A diplomatic action or expression in which a government follows precisely the same course or employs identical forms with reference to two or more other governments.

insurgent One who acts contrary to the policies and decisions of one's own political party.

intransigence Refusal to compromise or to abandon an extreme position or attitude.

machine A highly organized political group under the leadership of a boss or small clique.

manifest destiny An ostensibly benevolent or necessary policy of imperialistic expansion.

muckraker One who searches out and publicly exposes real or apparent misconduct of a prominent individual or business.

pecuniary Consisting of or measured in money.

propagandist One engaged in spreading a belief or ideas, facts, or allegations furthering one's cause or damaging an opposing cause.

protectorate The relationship of superior authority assumed by one power or state over a dependent political unit.

referendum The principle or practice of submitting to popular vote a measure passed on or proposed by a legislative body or by popular initiative.

reparation Compensation in money or materials payable by a defeated country for damages to or expenditures sustained by another country as a result of hostilities with the defeated country.

social Gospel A religious social-reform movement that was prominent from about 1870 to 1920, especially among liberal Protestant groups dedicated to the betterment of industrialized society through application of the biblical principles of charity and justice.

standpatter One who opposes or resists change.

subterfuge A deceptive device or stratagem.

tariff A schedule of duties imposed by a government on imported or, in some countries, exported goods.

tort A wrongful act other than a breach of contract for which relief may be obtained in the form of damages or an injunction.

trust A combination of firms or corporations formed by a legal agreement.

ukase A proclamation by a Russian emperor or government having the force of law.

yellow journalism The use of lurid features and sensationalized news in newspaper publishing to attract readers and increase circulation.

BIBLIOGRAPHY

OVERVIEWS

Informative general histories of the period include T. Jackson Lears, *Rebirth of a Nation: The Making of Modern America, 1877–1920* (2009); John Whiteclay Chambers, *The Tyranny of Change: America in the Progressive Era, 1890–1920*, 2nd ed. (2000); and H.W. Brands, *The Reckless Decade: America in the 1890s* (1995). Robert H. Wiebe, *The Search for Order, 1877–1920* (1967); and Richard Hostadter, *Age of Reform: From Bryan to F.D.R.* (1955), remain invaluable resources.

IMPERIALISM

John C. Bradford (ed.), *Crucible of Empire: The Spanish-American War and Its Aftermath* (1993); Walter LaFeber, *The Cambridge History of American Foreign Relations: The American Search for Opportunity, 1865–1913*, vol. 2 (1993); and Thomas J. McCormick, *China Market: America's Quest for Informal Empire, 1893–1901* (1967), examine American imperialism in several contexts.

PROGRESSIVISM

Ronald J. Pestritto and William J. Atto (eds.), *American Progressivism* (2008); Michael McGerr, *A Fierce Discontent: The Rise and Fall of the Progressive Movement in America, 1870–1920* (2003);

Glenda Elizabeth Gilmore (ed.), *Who Were the Progressives?* (2002); Daniel Rodgers, *Atlantic Crossings: Social Politics in a Progressive Age* (1998); and Arthur S. Link and Richard L. McCormick, *Progressivism* (1983), consider Progressivism and the Progressive era.

BIOGRAPHIES AND SPECIAL TOPICS

Among the engaging biographies of some of the period's leading figures are John Milton Cooper, *The Warrior and the Priest* (1983), comparing Woodrow Wilson and Theodore Roosevelt; Edmund Morris, *The Rise of Theodore Roosevelt* (1979), *Theodore Rex* (2001), and *Colonel Roosevelt* (2010); Daniel Levine, *Jane Addams and the Liberal Tradition* (1971, reprinted 1980); and Bernard A. Weisberger, *The La Follettes of Wisconsin: Love and Politics in Progressive America* (1994). Useful examinations of special topics include Glenn Porter, *The Rise of Big Business: 1860–1920* (2006); Alan M. Kraut, *The Huddled Masses: The Immigrant in American Society, 1880–1921*, 2nd ed (2001); John F. Kasson, *Amusing the Millions: Coney Island at the Turn of the Century* (1978); Martin J. Sklar, *The Corporate Reconstruction of American Capitalism, 1890–1916: The Market, the Law, and Politics*; and David Kennedy, *Over Here: The First World War and American Society*, 25th anniversary ed. (2004).